3.6.74

Feeling Alive After 65

Robert B. Taylor, M.D.

Feeling Alive After 65

The Complete Medical Guide for
Senior Citizens and Their Families

ARLINGTON HOUSE·PUBLISHERS

81 CENTRE AVENUE • NEW ROCHELLE, N. Y. 10801

MANUFACTURED IN THE UNITED STATES OF AMERICA

Library of Congress Cataloging in Publication Data

Taylor, Robert B
   Feeling alive after 65.

   Bibliography: p.
   1. Aged--Care and hygiene. I. Title.
[DNLM: 1. Geriatrics--Popular works. WT120
T245f 1974]
RC952.T38   615'.0438   73-13865
ISBN 0-87000-226-0

1793183

Grow old along with me!
The best is yet to be,
The last of life, for which
the first was made.
Robert Browning
(1812–1889)

Old age isn't so bad when
you consider the alternative.
Maurice Chevalier
(1889–1972)

Contents

Preface

Welcome to the Golden Years! This is the time you have worked and saved for—time to spend with the family, travel, read, or just go fishing.

But wait! Will arthritis limit travel? Will failing vision blur the pages of books? Or will a demanding bladder interrupt sleep? The Golden Years are not so golden if health fails.

Senior Citizen, now is the time to take stock of your most precious possession—health! Because you have passed the 65th milestone, your body is undergoing changes of aging that could lead to illness. Minor complaints arise—aches and pains that you never had before. Some will be subtle or imaginary and require only reassurance. But be wary! That petty pain may be the first sign of serious illness, the tip of the iceberg above the surface. What's hidden below?

In my medical practice, I have enjoyed the challenge of caring for the senior citizen. The emeritus scholar who wears a coat and tie to my office on the hottest summer day, the elderly woodworker who carves little animals for his grandchildren, and the retired housewife who brings the office staff cookies at Christmas—all present problems in medical care. The elderly scholar has a fantasy that he has cancer, but can't admit his fear lest it turn out to be true. What a service the family and physician can perform for this man by sensing and erasing his apprehension. The elderly woodworker fears a stroke; he knows his father and his brother suffered strokes, and with one arm limp, could he enjoy his life and hobbies? Diet changes, regular blood pressure checks, and knowledge of the nature of stroke could be of immense value to this man. The retired housewife fears loneliness; she's anxious and doesn't know why. She needs insight and doesn't know where to turn. All of these persons need to understand the changes of aging and how they set the stage for the physical and emotional problems of the senior citizen.

With advancing years, surviving the heart attacks and strokes of the sixties and seventies, some senior citizens will become unable to live independently at home. At this time the family needs guidance in the various techniques and devices necessary to care for an elderly invalid patient. How many middle-aged daughters have given a bedpan or made a bed with the patient lying in it? How many people know how to turn a sleeping patient in bed easily?

When illness precludes home care, facilities in the hospital and the nursing home must be evaluated. The emotional reaction of the family members must be considered, and a sometimes difficult decision must be made as to where the elderly infirm patient can receive the best level of care.

Feeling Alive After 65 is a manual for those who have passed their 65th birthday and wish to understand the changes going on inside their bodies. There are chapters concerning retirement, nutrition, and diseases common after age 65. The drug and diet therapy of many diseases is discussed, with specific medications and diet programs outlined as general examples rather than specific recommendations. Parts of the book are also a guide for the family that loves and will care for the senior citizen in his later years, with advice on the care of the invalid elderly at home, in the hospital, in the nursing home, and during his final hours.

Feeling Alive After 65 embodies information, advice, facts, and sometimes opinions concerning how to prevent disease and preserve vitality during the Golden Years.

Good health is your most valuable asset. Let's work together to protect it!

Acknowledgments

Bouquets to the typists—Mary Ellen Rebhan, Mary Ann Fischler, Carol Ostmark, and Patricia McCann—veterans of the many manuscript drafts peppered with additions, corrections, and margin notes. Three cheers for Royal S. Davis, M.D., whose comments and stern criticism guided the final manuscript revision; and for Herbert M. Weinman, M.D., who capably cared for my patients while their usual doctor satisfied the itch to write.

Applause for my favorite senior citizens, Mr. and Mrs. O. C. Taylor, who offered encouragement from first page to last index entry.

And a quiet thank you to my wife, Anita, and my daughters, Diana and Sharon, who sharpened pencils, corrected spelling, and gave Daddy the time he needed to finish the book.

Feeling
Alive After
65

Cheerful Todays and Confident Tomorrows

*The true way to render age vigorous is to
prolong the youth of the mind.*
MORTIMER COLLINS
(1827-1876)

DON'T FEAR ADVANCING AGE

Aging is changing. Indeed, your whole life has been one of change,
beginning at birth, reaching a peak of strength and vigor in your
twenties and thirties, and continuing over the past thirty-odd years to
the seasoned maturity of the senior citizen. Let's stop and consider
your attitude toward the advancing years and the changes of aging.

Many of the so-called ills of the advancing years can be corrected
by a change in outlook. The years past 65 must be considered a time of
harvest, when you can relax and enjoy the fruits of a lifetime of hard
work. The senior citizen assumes his rightful place as an elder whose
advice is respected (if not always followed), yet he is spared many of
the cravings, worries, and responsibilities of the younger members of
the family.

ADAPTING TO RETIREMENT

Retirement is a commencement—the beginning of a new phase of life,
with the opportunity to explore new interests and hobbies that, until

now, have been neglected for want of leisure time. Indeed, retirement brings a wealth of time, which must be carefully budgeted to balance hours for hobbies, recreation, rest, travel, and duties at home.

A 68-year-old patient visited my office complaining of extreme fatigue; let's call him Mr. Johnson. "Doctor, I drag myself out of bed tired in the morning, run out of steam trying to perform a few household duties, nap in the afternoon after lunch, but then, however I try, I can't fall asleep at night." And poor Mrs. Johnson! She complained, "My husband hasn't enough pep to go shopping or even to work in the garden. He is always tired." Upon further questioning, the patient mentioned a poor appetite, slight weight loss, and a feeling that his life had no purpose.

A careful physical examination, including a chest X ray and examination of the blood and urine, failed to show any evidence of physical illness. Further discussion revealed the fact that Mr. Johnson had retired three years ago without having made preparation for the burden of idle time, with the mistaken idea that "retirement is just a long vacation."

A sedentary vacation can be a shot in the arm for the busy executive who can leave work for a week or two and lie in the sun, glad to be rid of responsibility. The human mind, however, can tolerate only short periods of such inactivity; if the "vacation" is prolonged, boredom leads to fatigue. Mr. Johnson had never played golf or fished; he had no hobbies, had not read a book in ten years, and was mentally prepared to spend his remaining years on the living room sofa, staring at the television set.

My treatment of Mr. Johnson's condition included setting the alarm to arise every day at 7:00 A.M., rather than snoozing until midmorning. A project was planned for each day: cleaning out the garage, trimming the hedges, building a bird feeder, painting a chair, or going to the library to borrow a book. The afternoon nap was strictly forbidden, since daytime rest is often followed by nighttime wakefulness. A twice-weekly outing to a local place of interest was prescribed; soon Mr. Johnson was taking his wife to visit nearby museums, historical sites, and picnic groves, all within a short distance of home. Television was limited to one hour of selected viewing during the day, and the patient was encouraged to read in the evening before retiring.

The Johnsons joined the Senior Citizens' Club and participated in its regular meetings and outings. Before long, Mr. Johnson was elected club treasurer and spent a few hours each week keeping the books in order. Mr. and Mrs. Johnson joined the drive for local low-cost senior citizen housing and found that, by attending town board meetings and buttonholing politicians, senior citizens could push through needed legislation.

When examined in my office three months after beginning treatment, Mr. Johnson reported, "I feel better than I have in years." He was more vigorous and was taking increasing pride in his home repairs and Senior Citizens' Club activities. He had developed an interest in ceramics after taking a course with the local adult education program and asked if his next appointment might be postponed several weeks because he and his wife were joining a Senior Citizens' Club trip to Mexico to study native art.

The vigorous life can keep you young long after you receive your Medicare card. To preserve your continued good health, however, don't forget the value of preventive medicine and the advice of your family physician. His counsel, plus creative interests and sound health habits, can keep you feeling alive after 65.

To Guard
Is Better Than
to Heal

And lo! The starry folds reveal
The blazoned truth we hold so dear:
To guard is better than to heal,
The shield is nobler than the spear!
OLIVER WENDELL HOLMES
(1809-1894)

Preserving vitality and avoiding disease—that's what this book is all about. Doctors call it preventive medicine and, after 65, the availability and quality of local health care may become all-important. Let's look at the services available and how they can keep you feeling fit.

CHOOSE A FAMILY DOCTOR BEFORE ILLNESS STRIKES

"Doctor, I'm not sick. But I would like to make an appointment for a checkup, so we can get acquainted." The choice of a family doctor, like choosing a spouse, is one of the most important decisions of your life. Your relationship with your family doctor should be so close and continuing that you feel free to call on him for advice even on matters that seem trivial. The compassionate family physician, realizing that peace of mind is one of the greatest gifts that he has to offer, will patiently explain the reasons for your complaints.

Select your family doctor with care. Don't make the mistake of consulting the state medical directory and choosing the physician

5

having the most letters after his name. Many fine hardworking physicians shun the practice of collecting postgraduate degree letters and concentrate on providing top patient care.

Perhaps your best source of advice in choosing a family physician is a person whose work brings him in contact with local doctors, such as a pharmacist, nurse, or pharmaceutical salesman. These professionals are familiar with the doctor's credentials and his reputation in the medical community. A call to the nurse on duty at the emergency room of the hospital will provide you with the names of two or three family physicians in your area, and she will very likely select those whom she knows to be hardworking and capable. The county medical society will be glad to furnish you with names of family physicians in your neighborhood.

It's not easy for the patient to examine the credentials of a prospective doctor. Perhaps this is just as well. Many excellent family physicians are graduates of lesser known medical colleges, and it is said that the prestigious medical schools often channel their best men into research. There is a medical honor society called Alpha Omega Alpha, and membership in this society is a plus in your doctor's favor. The American Medical Association gives a physician's achievement award for continuing education; this small certificate hanging on the doctor's wall testifies that he has taken an impressive number of refresher courses. A part-time teaching position at a local hospital shows that his professional colleagues consider your prospective physician's knowledge to be above average.

Many family physicians have taken the examination for accreditation by the American Board of Family Practice. This is a backbreaking two-day test, the successful completion of which signifies that the doctor is qualified to offer above-average care in all phases of medicine. No physician who has failed to keep up with recent advances in medical care will be able to pass; a certificate that your prospective physician is a Diplomate of the American Board of Family Practice is a sign of merit.

Always choose a family physician who is on the staff of the hospital you wish to use if you become ill. Virtually all family physicians are on hospital staffs; it takes only a phone call to the prospective physician's nurse to determine which hospital he attends.

Some communities, particularly larger cities, have a shortage of capable family physicians; if this is the case, your next choice should be an internist: a specialist in the diagnosis and treatment of disease. The internist does not treat children and does not perform surgery of any kind, however minor. The internist is a highly trained specialist often called in consultation to supplement care by the family physician.

Finally, let's look at other considerations before choosing your family physician. Is there public transportation near his office? If you drive, is there adequate parking? Will another doctor take his calls when he is out of town? Can he be reached at the office for a telephone consultation? Will he make house calls if you are too sick to come to the office? Most important, are his patients satisfied with the quality of the medical care that they are receiving?

KNOW YOUR HOSPITAL

It's a good idea to learn about your local hospital, since it may some day play a vital role in your health. Virtually all hospitals have open-house or fund-raising functions that give you an opportunity to get acquainted, and the hospital gift shop, with good ideas for birthday and Christmas gifts, is open to anyone who wishes to shop there. Just as the expectant father will sometimes make a practice run of his route to the hospital, so you should be aware of the location of your hospital and how to get there in an emergency. The telephone number of the hospital should be posted by the bedside, together with the numbers of your family doctor and local ambulance. Perhaps your hospital has an ambulance service; your community may have a commercial ambulance on 24-hour call. In smaller communities, there may be a volunteer ambulance or rescue squad that, with a well-trained and enthusiastic crew, is often the equal of professional ambulance service.

Within the hospital you should know the location and facilities of the emergency room. Will they be able to care for your needs if your doctor is out of town? Since your doctor may send you to the hospital for X rays, you should note the location of the X-ray department. Does that department have a division of nuclear medicine, a recent medical development that allows studies of various organs with tracer or radio-active-tagged particles? The hospital laboratory is also used by doctors in the community; you should be aware of its location and the facilities available to you.

Does your hospital have an intensive-care unit? In this division, another hospital innovation of the last two decades, the most seriously ill patients receive care. The intensive-care unit has up-to-date electronic devices for following heartbeat, respiration, and temperature that give an instant warning of any change in the patient's condition, along with the latest equipment for resuscitation in the event of a sudden emergency. All modern hospitals today have such a unit.

Visiting sick friends in the hospital allows a peek at the rooms. Are there ward accommodations with many beds in an open area, or are there comfortable, airy semiprivate rooms? Are the rooms air-conditioned for comfort in the summer? Is there an intercom system that enables the patient to speak directly to the nurse without having to summon her to the bedside with a buzzer? Are the beds electrically operated, with accessible hand controls that allow the patient to raise and lower the bed without calling the nurse?

Lastly, is your hospital accredited by the Joint Commission on Hospital Accreditation, and is the hospital approved by the Social Security Administration for Medicare payments?

YOUR MOST IMPORTANT HOUR

Every person past the age of 40 should have a regular annual physical examination. Scheduling the examination on your birthdate may help you to remember it.

Conscientious family physicians welcome the opportunity to perform a periodic health survey on their patients as a means of preventing illness. A physician who is too busy to perform a comprehensive health examination may be too busy to provide your family with top-quality medical care. However, because there is a demand for complete physical examinations and because you should be in no acute distress at this time, make your appointment several weeks in advance. At least one hour should be allowed for the examination, and perhaps more, depending on the procedure in your doctor's office.

When you report for your examination, the secretary will record your name, address, phone number, and other data. The office nurse will measure your height and weight and test your vision, and many offices will also perform an audiometric hearing test. A complete urinalysis will be done. The office technician will draw blood for examination.

The doctor will question you concerning complaints, both present and past. He will discuss your medical history and operations, and he will make a careful record of the illnesses of your mother, father, brothers, sisters, and other family members. You will be questioned concerning your habits of smoking, alcohol, and coffee. Your doctor will want to know any medications that you are taking regularly and any allergies to drugs or food.

The doctor will check you literally from top to toe. He will measure your blood pressure, examine your eyes, including the retina at the back of the eye, look in your ears, nose, and throat, examine your neck and thyroid gland, listen to your chest and heart, palpate your abdomen, check the males for hernia, and do an internal examination with a Pap test for females. A rectal examination is an important part of the checkup. Reflexes will be tested, and the circulation to the feet will be examined.

In a completely equipped office, the technician will next perform an electrocardiogram, a record of the electric activity controlling the heart muscle. A chest X ray, indispensable in a thorough physical examination, will be performed; prompt developing allows a reading within minutes.

After the tests are completed, you and the doctor will sit down together in his consultation room to discuss any problems he has found. The doctor will advise you about your habits and prescribe any medication needed. He will recommend that you return in one year for your next annual physical examination; if any problems have been found, he will advise you to return during the interval for periodic examinations.

PERIODIC HEALTH CHECKUPS

Many persons over 65 have some medical problem requiring regular care by the family physician. The blood pressure may be a little above normal and require medication; fluid may pool in the ankles each evening, requiring diuretics; or mild diabetes may require regulation of the diet and medication. Corpulence calls for supervision of the diet. A regular visit at one- to three-month intervals will enable the physician to follow the weight, blood pressure, heart rate, and other physical signs and allow analysis of the urine for sugar and other abnormalities. The goal of periodic health checkups is detection of disease before it becomes a serious problem.

At your periodic examination, the doctor will discuss preventive measures to build defenses against illness. Flu shots are very important for persons over 65 or for those with chronic illness. Elderly persons with a poor appetite and limited diet should take supplementary vitamins, and the prescription of iron tablets may be necessary for the prevention or treatment of an iron-deficiency anemia. Sugar in the urine may be the first hint of diabetes. Finally, the periodic visit to the doctor allows discussion of minor but possibly significant complaints without waiting for the annual physical examination.

THE WARNING SIGNS OF CANCER

Persons over 65 are in what is known as the cancer age group. In 1910, cancer was the sixth most common cause of death, trailing behind cardiovascular diseases and four different infectious illnesses. Giant strides in antibiotic therapy have caused infections to retreat, bringing cancer to second place, surpassed only by cardiovascular disease as the leading cause of death in the United States today.

Cancer is a growth of new tissue called a tumor; a malignant tumor can spread from one part of the body to another. While the exact cause of cancer is still a mystery, investigators in countless laboratories are constantly at work to determine its cause and the reasons for its spread. Breakthroughs in the treatment of cancer will follow as we run down the clues that will reveal the actual basis of the disease.

Many people who die of cancer could have been saved by prompt detection and therapy. Of every six people who develop cancer, two are cured by present modes of treatment: surgery, X ray, and chemotherapy; three are considered incurable by present methods of treatment; and one was curable, but will die of his disease because of delayed detection and therapy! These latter cases might have been saved through regular physical examinations and reporting to their doctor the presence of the danger signs of cancer.

There are seven well-known warning signs of cancer:

Persistent cough and hoarseness may herald a cancer of the throat, larynx, or lung and should prompt the physician to examine the lungs, throat, and larynx. A chest X ray should be taken.

Persistent change in bowel or bladder habits may be the first sign of cancer of the large intestine, rectum, bladder, or prostate. The symptoms may be inability to pass urine, persistent diarrhea, or constipation. Blood in the urine, burning upon urination, or blood in the bowel movement should all prompt immediate medical attention.

Persistent indigestion or difficulty in swallowing may signal cancer of the throat, esophagus, or stomach. Recurrent vomiting, belching, heartburn, inability to digest certain foods, and similar symptoms will be the signal for the doctor to order complete X rays of the stomach and intestinal tract.

Unusual bleeding or discharge from any part of the body, including ears, nose, throat, penis, vagina, rectum, or other areas can be an ominous sign. No recurrent bleeding should be ignored, and any persistent discharge should be promptly reported to the physician.

A lump or thickening in the breast or elsewhere may signal a tumor of breast tissue or an enlarged lymph gland. These are often removed surgically for diagnosis. Of those removed, most do not turn out to be cancerous; however, a small but significant number are malignant. There is a high percentage of cures in those cases that are detected early.

A change in a wart or mole may be the first sign of malignant change. A particularly vicious cancer called malignant melanoma can arise from an otherwise harmless mole; early detection allows local removal of the cancer, sometimes even in the doctor's office. Delay can end in radical surgery, and sometimes cure is not possible.

A sore that does not heal is the cardinal sign of cancer of the skin. Skin cancer, which accounts for 17 per cent of all cancers, is completely curable if detected early.

IMMUNIZATIONS TO PROTECT YOUR HEALTH

In 1884, Louis Pasteur wrote, "When meditating over a disease, I never think of finding a remedy for it, but, instead, a means of preventing it."

Immunization involves the injection of small amounts of weakened disease organisms that, when they enter the system, induce the body to produce antibodies that attack this foreign material. The antibodies may stay in the bloodstream for years, acting as sentinels against future invasion by similar bacteria.

Flu shots are considered very important for persons over 65. The 1918 flu epidemic caused millions of deaths, both by the disease itself and by such complications as pneumonia. Flu-related disabilities and deaths can be greatly reduced by taking preventive flu shots in the fall and early winter to maintain a high antibody level during the danger months. I routinely give my older patients two injections, the first in late September, October, or early November, and the second booster injection about Christmastime.

Worried about a "reaction"? The highly refined vaccines now available minimize the sick feeling that the older, less pure, flu shots once caused. Statistical data accumulated over the last ten years indicate that shots provide a good, but not perfect, protection against the flu virus.

The older person should keep up his immunizations against diphtheria, tetanus, and polio. These immunizations become due every four years, and a review of their need should be part of your annual physical examination.

Smallpox vaccination, typhoid shots, and cholera, typhus, and yellow fever inoculations are required only for those persons planning to travel outside the United States. Requirements vary in each country.

Poison ivy shots are available to persons whose hobby is gardening or landscaping and who have shown an unusual sensitivity to the resin of this common weed. Poison ivy is a serious problem in many wooded areas of the country. Severe attacks may occur even in midwinter when there are no leaves on the vines to allow recognition, but when the sap is present in the dormant plant. Poison ivy vines on firewood present a common source of winter infection. The poison ivy shots consist of four immunizations at one-week intervals the first year; one booster dose administered in April or May each subsequent year suffices for continued protection. Although these injections increase resistance to poison ivy, lack of scrupulous cleanliness following gardening can still lead to an occasional rash.

Cold shots, a mixture of various bacteria known to cause respiratory infections, are sometimes recommended for older persons who suffer from frequent colds and later complications. There is considerable controversy over the effectiveness of cold shots; while some preparations have been removed from the market, patients who have taken them regularly insist that they are helpful.

YOUR HOME MEDICINE CABINET

The home medicine cabinet should contain simple remedies for common minor illnesses, but should not become a repository for an assortment of outdated and unlabeled medications. All antibiotics have an expiration date, known to the druggist, but unknown to you. For this reason, your doctor will usually prescribe antibiotics to be taken for a short but definite period of time, to be used completely with none left over. Digitalis, diuretics, quinidine, tranquilizers, and most other medicines used on a regular basis have no expiration date and can be refilled as instructed by the doctor. When your doctor prescribes a cough medicine or a decongestant for a cold, be sure to ask him if this remedy can be used in the future for simple coughs and colds.

The up-to-date medicine cabinet should contain the following items in addition to prescription medicine: aspirin or buffered aspirin for headache or simple viral illness; a mild laxative such as milk of magnesia; and one-quarter per cent Neo-Synephrine nose drops for nasal congestion. With your doctor's approval, a patent medicine such as Dristan or Contac for the common cold may be kept on hand. Simple lozenges for mild sore throats are helpful, and an antacid such as Maalox to relieve mild gastric distress may be used at infrequent intervals. Simple decongestant eyedrops such as Visine help to relieve sore, itching eyes, an over-the-counter cough medicine such as Cheracol may calm a tickling cough, and Kaopectate may be a life-saver when transient diarrhea strikes. Most mild symptoms may be treated safely with these medications for several days, but increasing severity or prolonged duration of complaints means it's time to call the doctor.

A Plan
for Careful
Living

*Accident—an inevitable occurrence due to
the action of immutable natural laws.*
AMBROSE BIERCE
(1842-1914)

Avoiding mishaps is essential to feeling alive (or even staying alive) after
65. Here's how.

MOST ACCIDENTS OCCUR AT HOME

Accidents are often preventable. Each year, perhaps on the day of
your annual physical examination, walk slowly through your home
and appraise each room critically for possible danger areas. Remember that you are likely to be visited by other senior citizens who may
not have your keen eye and your knowledge of where the floor is
slippery, the carpet is loose, or the electric cord may trip. Good
health at this time is too precious to be risked, and all areas of
potential danger should be repaired promptly.

Many home accidents occur from a long-standing oversight of
habit, placement, or misuse, and physical injury could have been
prevented if the error had been recognized and corrected. Awkward
furniture placement, heavy items stored on high shelves, and deteriorating electrical devices represent inconveniences to younger persons

with sharp eyes and quick reflexes, but are deadly hazards to older citizens with failing vision, slower reflexes, and arthritic hands. Heavy items should be stored within easy reach; if you must stretch for something stored high, be sure to bring a sturdy stepladder and take your time retrieving the item. Avoid major repairs, particularly those involving mechanical devices. Smoking in bed can end your days in a burst of flame.

Clothes can cause accidents. Loose-fitting slippers without heels can snag rugs or furniture, causing a serious tumble, while garments with hanging belts or ties may catch on doorknobs or handles. Loose or torn carpets should be replaced immediately, and scatter rugs—threats waiting for a time and victim—should be discarded. Furniture that blocks a path of traffic should be pushed to another location. Stairs should be inspected for torn carpeting or slippery spots, and firm handrails should be installed, if not already present.

Electric cords must be arranged so that there is no chance of their snaring an unwary foot. A night light should glow in the bedroom so that, if you arise before dawn, you are not in total darkness. One lamp in the home should be attached to an inexpensive electric timer that automatically turns it on in the afternoon and off after bedtime; the timer will function even in your absence and help discourage burglars.

The bathroom should be inspected for possible sites of injury. The bathtub should have firm handholds at both a high and lower level. The bottom of the tub should be covered with a skidproof material to avoid a fall, and carpeting in the bathroom may prevent skidding on slippery tiles.

FIRE PRECAUTIONS

Fire represents a special threat to older persons whose sense of smell and reflexes are not as acute as they were a decade ago. Walk through your home and plan at least two exits from each room—both the normal exit and an emergency escape hatch such as a window. If the bedroom lacks a fire escape, one should be constructed now.

Important fire precautions include use of large ashtrays, prompt disposal of all rubbish or cleaning rags, avoidance of overloading electric circuits, and use of an asbestos tray on the ironing board. The number of the fire department should be posted near all telephone extensions.

MACHINERY CAN BE HAZARDOUS

The older person's diminished physical strength, reduced coordination, and decreased vision may make the use of machinery and power tools hazardous. Modern gadgets save many hours of toil, but they can also do instant and irreparable damage to the body. The stove and cooktop must be handled with extra care by senior citizens; the electric carving knife can saw through a finger as well as slice a rib roast.

Older men must have respect for power tools. The electric drill, the lathe, and the power saw that have served so well over the years become increasingly hazardous after age 65. Electric hedge clippers can cause serious injury to fingers and can cause electric damage if the clipper snips the trailing cord. Power mowers have amputated many toes; a chain saw can cut through a hand or leg as quickly as it can cut through a tree limb. Modern contrivances can compensate for reduced strength after 65, but they must be handled with scrupulous care if injuries are to be prevented.

SHOULD YOU DRIVE A CAR?

*Until Homo Sapiens becomes more sapient, I can
see no prospect of his ever ... learning that
two automobiles cannot occupy the same spot at
the same time, especially when they come from
opposite directions.*
EVARTS A. GRAHAM
(1883-1957)

Every person over the age of 65 should periodically ask himself the question, "Should I drive a car?" Indeed, your insurance company will very likely be asking this question of you and your doctor. Law-enforcement officers and judges will ask the same question if you become involved in an accident. No matter how spry and robust you feel, you must concede that your reactions and strength are not as capable as they were in the days when television was new and pot was something you cooked in.

Medications, often those taken by older persons, are of considerable concern to law-enforcement officers and insurance companies. Drugs that can alter alertness include tranquilizers, certain blood-pressure depressants, sleeping pills, antihistamines, some ingredients in cough medicines, muscle relaxants, a few medications taken for abdominal distress, and a host of others. Law-enforcement officials consider driving while under the influence of a medication similar to driving under the influence of alcohol; it behooves the senior citizen taking medication to ask his doctor or pharmacist whether the medication may impair alertness.

Any condition that causes or may cause periods of unconsciousness should be adequate reason to stop driving. Heart attacks, fainting, small strokes, or severe angina may cause sudden loss of consciousness; if such an attack occurs while driving, the patient may suffer a serious accident.

Senior citizens with disabling arthritis, weakness of a limb, or severe deformity may not be capable of operating a motor vehicle safely. Sometimes, when the older person has suffered subtle mental changes that make him incapable of determining his ability to operate an automobile, his family must make this decision for him. If the doctor gives his approval to stay behind the wheel for another year, the over-65 driver must obey these rules of the road:

Avoid turnpike driving. Expressway driving, a specialized type of motoring that calls for youthful alertness and lightning reflexes, should be left to younger persons. The senior driver should take the scenic route with less congested roads.

Don't drive unless well rested and in good health. The driver who falls asleep at the wheel may awake in the hospital.

Do not drive too slow or too fast. Many serious accidents are caused as an impatient driver rushes past a slowpoke. When the accident occurs, the slowpoke moseys on, never realizing he was the cause.

Use your safety devices—seatbelts and shoulder harnesses. Form the habit of buckling up before reaching for the ignition key.

Keep your car in good condition with regular checkups, inspecting tires, headlights, brakes, and windshield wipers at frequent intervals.

Avoid long trips. Remember that your endurance is less than it was 20 years ago. Plan shorter trips with frequent rest stops.

When asked by an older patient if he is fit to drive, I ask him to consider this question, "If your grandchild ran in front of your car, could you stop in time?" If the answer is no, then my patient understands why he should surrender his operator's license.

An Asthma
and a
Dropsy

My diseases are an asthma and a dropsy,
and what is less curable, seventy-five.
SAMUEL JOHNSON
(1709-1784)

THE AGING PROCESS

Old machines wear out. Today there are few cars on the road more than ten years old, and factories replace equipment every five to ten years. Of course, machines don't suddenly fall apart; they wear out piece by piece. Tires wear thin, the gearshift sticks, valves become sluggish, and the exhaust system rusts through. Part after part wears out and is mended until it no longer becomes practicable to continue repair, and the machine is replaced by a newer model.

The body ages in the same fashion, with a gradual deterioration of valves, wires, hinges, and plumbing. Some organs show wear and tear before others; when the aging process becomes sufficiently advanced, there is a breakdown in the organ system called disease. Joints that have gradually worn down become painful. The lens of the eye grows cloudy, with progressively dimming vision. Day by day, hardening of the arteries squeezes off blood flow to the heart and brain, necessitating a higher blood pressure to supply vital organs. One by one, the aging organ systems show evidence of breakdown, and these problems are brought to the doctor for repair or replacement. Your personal physician, with the discoveries of modern medicine at his command, will continually repair ailing organ systems as long as they are capable of sustaining the aging machine.

HABITS BEGIN TO SHOW

"Habit is a sort of second nature," wrote Cicero, and after 65 your body will begin to reflect the habits of decades. Have you regularly provided your body with adequate nutrition, exercise, and rest? Or have you wantonly indulged yourself with excessive alcohol, tobacco, and food? Now is the time when your good health habits will be rewarded and your excesses become cause for regret.

Overeating is a vice. I have known many delightful overweight ladies who would be most disdainful of the alcoholic, yet who are hopelessly addicted to chocolate cake. Every extra pound of body fat contains miles of capillaries that the heart must supply. Chronic obesity contributes to a host of diseases, including diabetes, chronic backache, arthritis, and hypertension.

Jerome K. Jerome wrote, "We drink one another's health and spoil our own." Alcohol anesthetizes brain cells and acts as a poison to the liver. It has a slight beneficial effect of opening up the capillaries, and the temperate use of alcohol, not more than one or two drinks a day, probably presents no health hazard other than the additional calories added to the diet. However, excessive use of alcohol over the years will lead to progressive malnutrition and chronic liver disease. The intemperate use of alcohol can aggravate diabetes, peptic ulcer, and emotional problems.

Tobacco has no useful function in man or animals. The use of tobacco has a cumulative effect over a lifetime, and the end result may be chronic lung disease or cancer of the lung, lip, tongue, or throat. All younger or middle-aged persons who hope to spend their later years without the tragedy of emphysema or cancer should immediately cease the use of tobacco.

Overwork is a contributing factor in many of the illnesses of old age. The person who has systematically worked too many hours a day too many days a week for too many years may be penalized by increased hardening of the arteries and an elevated blood pressure. There is an increased incidence of peptic ulcer and colitis in persons who take their work and worries home each night. We should each restrict our work week to five days, with adequate time off for relaxation.

IMPROVE YOUR POSTURE

Good posture increases the expansion of the lungs, increases the volume of blood pumped by each heartbeat, and helps prevent fatigue. Most cases of chronic backache can be traced back to improper habits of posture, with incorrect lifting, bending, carrying, sitting, and standing. Pay attention to your posture! Walk tall with your head up as though you were trying to brush the ceiling with your hair. When seated, rest your back by crossing the knees. Don't slouch. Lift correctly by keeping your back straight and bending your knees, using your heavy leg muscles to lift. Stand erect and you ease the strain on the muscles and ligaments of the lower back.

Obesity is the enemy of good posture. A protuberant abdomen causes a swayback stance because the shoulders must be thrown back to counterbalance the large paunch. Swayback posture, in turn, is a common cause of chronic backache.

Exercise daily to improve your posture. A long walk with the head erect and the shoulders back helps to bring air deep into the lungs. A good exercise for improving posture is to stand with your back to the wall, touching the heels, buttocks, shoulders, and back of the head to the wall. Stand straight, lift your chest about an inch, then inhale and exhale ten times slowly. Performing this exercise four times a day will help to improve posture and give you an increased sense of vitality.

THE IMPORTANCE OF EXERCISE

Dr. Paul Dudley White, the renowned heart specialist who treated President Eisenhower, stresses the importance of exercise in maintaining muscle tone, improving blood circulation, and preventing hypertension, heart attacks, and stroke. In his autobiography, *My Life and Medicine,* Dr. White writes, "The difficulty of our way of life is that man no longer labors much, and so must substitute exercise for the former necessity of working hard physically."

Regular physical exercise helps prevent chronic fatigue by tightening muscles and promoting restful sleep. Many persons complaining of insomnia in reality suffer from a lack of exercise, going to bed each night with bodies that have not been exercised sufficiently during the day to require more than a few hours' sleep at night. Carefully controlled studies have shown that regular physical exercise will lower serum cholesterol, helping to prevent hardening of the arteries. Exercise, of course, burns up excessive calories and can bolster a lagging appetite. The veins in the legs need regular exercise for proper function, and the bowel becomes sluggish when the body is inactive.

The senior citizen should consult his personal physician for the specific exercises most appropriate to his physical condition. The doctor's advice may include one or more of the following:

Deep breathing exercises, to increase aeration of the lungs and strengthen chest muscles, should be performed daily by all persons past 65. Stand erect with the shoulders back and the head held high. Inhale deeply and exhale ten times, with each inward breath extending the arms out to the side and lowering them with exhalation.

The back can be strengthened by touching the toes, bending forward from the waist and coming as close as possible to the toes, then rising slowly, placing the hands on hips. Repeat this exercise ten times daily. If backache is a problem, omit toe-touching and go on to the next exercise.

The muscles of the abdominal wall, which often sag after age 40, can be strengthened by situps. Lie flat on the floor, with hands over your head. Rise to a sitting position, reaching forward to touch the toes, then slowly lie back flat again. Repeat this exercise five or ten times daily.

The thighs can be strengthened by sitting on the edge of a chair and extending the legs one at a time, raising the foot off the floor until it extends straight out from the chair. Repeat this exercise ten times daily with each leg.

The lower legs are strengthened by standing erect, arising from a flatfooted position to stand on your toes. Stand on your toes for a count of three, and then come down again. Repeat this exercise 15 times daily.

The shoulders and upper arms are strengthened by holding two fairly heavy books in the hands and raising the arms from the sides until they are straight up in the air, then returning the arms slowly to your side.

The upper arm muscles are developed by holding the books in front of the body; bend the elbows, bringing them up until held in front of the chest, then lowering to the side. Repeat each of these exercises ten times daily.

The wrists and hands are strengthened by forcefully bending and unbending the fingers. Repeat this exercise twenty times daily, perhaps while squeezing a rubber ball.

The reward of regular exercise is youthful muscle tone, increased vigor, a better night's sleep and, hopefully, longer life as the progress of aging is slowed.

The Mysteries of Diet

In general, mankind, since the improvement of cookery, eats twice as much as nature requires.

BENJAMIN FRANKLIN
(1706-1790)
Poor Richard's Almanack

EAT A BALANCED DIET

Food provides the raw materials for energy and replacement of worn-out cells. In a very real sense, you are what you eat. The type of food eaten and the patterns of eating are altered and the metabolism of nutrients undergoes subtle changes after age 65.

Proteins provide the building blocks for muscle, nerves, blood, connective tissue, and the fiber of bone. The chief sources of protein are meat, dairy products, and certain vegetables. A deficiency in protein intake will lead to shrinkage of muscles, weakening of the bones and, in very severe cases, bloating and mental deficiency.

Meats have long been a staple in the American diet, in contrast to most other countries of the world. The per capita intake of meat in the United States is more than twice that of Japan and twenty times that of Colombia, helping to give the average American a larger skeleton and more muscle than the average Japanese or Colombian. However, because meats are also high in fats and cholesterol, the average American has a much higher incidence of arteriosclerosis than his brothers around the world.

Fats add flavor to the diet; a fat-free diet is decidedly unpalatable. The chief sources of both fats and proteins are meat, dairy products, and some vegetables. Since fats are characterized by a high caloric value per given weight, in a weight-reduction diet fat intake must be severely trimmed. With very few exceptions, the various fatty acids are not required for human metabolism, and, because of the relationship of fats, cholesterol, and arteriosclerosis, the person over 65 should consume as little fat as possible in the diet.

Carbohydrates are fuel foods that, if unused, can be stored in the liver for future use. The chief sources of carbohydrates are cereals, bread, potatoes, and sugar. In the United States, carbohydrates provide about 45 per cent of the total daily caloric intake, but in many Asian and African nations cereal grains provide as much as 80 per cent of the day's calories.

Minerals are found in various amounts throughout the human body. Calcium, which requires vitamin D for metabolism, combines with phosphate in bones and teeth. Magnesium, copper, and cobalt are found in small amounts in the body, but perform important functions. Fluoride, although not yet shown to be indispensable in nutrition, has been found to aid in the prevention of dental cavities.

Although sodium chloride, common table salt, is present in large amounts in the blood and tissues, a high intake of salt can contribute to heart failure and high blood pressure. Because salt will draw water to it, excessive sodium chloride swells the fluid volume of the blood and puts an added strain on the heart. The heart beats faster and pumps at a higher pressure. If the salt content of the blood is too great and an excessive amount of water is present in the blood, the heart fails to pump the blood as fast as it returns to the veins, and heart failure begins.

Calories are a measurement of energy. Any portion of food can be metabolized to provide a certain amount of energy, measured in calories. One calorie is defined as the amount of heat required to raise the temperature of one gram of water one degree Centigrade. This same energy can move muscle or pump the heart or stimulate the brain to compose a poem. The food that provides the calories, if not used for energy, will be converted into storage forms such as body fat or liver glycogen.

The daily food intake should balance the daily activity, so that the number of calories produced by metabolism of food each day equals the number of calories burned in performing the daily chores. The average 25-year-old 150-pound American man leading a moderately active life requires about 2,800 calories daily. Persons over 65, usually less active than the vigorous 25-year-old, will require fewer calories—approximately 2,000 or less. If you are already overweight, your caloric intake should be reduced still further so that liver glycogen and fatty tissue are burned for energy.

In his message to Congress of February 21, 1963, on "The Problems of the Aged," John F. Kennedy said, "Too many elderly people with small incomes skimp on food at a time when their health requires greater quantity, variety, and balance in their diets." Elderly persons, often living alone, may suffer from poor appetite and be content with a diet of tea and toast and, unless supervised, may develop progressive malnutrition. The elderly person existing on a diet deficient in protein, vegetables, fruit, and vitamins may suffer extreme weakness, weight loss, anemia, and the signs of vitamin deficiency.

VITAMINS ARE IMPORTANT

Vitamins control vital chemical reactions within the body. They provide no calories themselves, but are required by the body to use the foodstuffs that have been eaten. A deficiency of certain vitamins can lead to complex disease pictures.

Vitamin A is important in vision, and a deficiency can cause night blindness and a scaling dry skin. The chief sources of vitamin A are green or yellow vegetables, liver, fish oils, eggs, milk, and butter. The recommended daily dietary allowance for adults is 5000-8000 units.

Vitamin B_1 (thiamine), active in the metabolism of carbohydrates and in nerve function, is found in yeast, whole grains, meat, and vegetables. A shortage of thiamine causes a weakness of the nerves called neuritis or beriberi. The recommended daily allowance of thiamine is 1-1.5 mg.

Vitamin B_2 (riboflavin), vital in the metabolism of many foods, is found in milk, cheese, liver, meats, and eggs. A deficiency of vitamin B_2 results in inflammation of the lips and mouth. The recommended daily dietary allowance of vitamin B_2 for adults is 1.5-2.0 mg.

Niacin is required for the metabolism of certain foods and to maintain normal intestinal and skin function. Niacin is found in wheat germ, yeast, organ meats, liver, and peanuts. Pellagra, the classic picture of niacin deficiency, involves inflammation of the skin, diarrhea, sore tongue, and mental deterioration. The daily adult dietary allowance of niacin is 17-21 mg.

Vitamin B_6 (pyridoxine), active in the metabolism of certain proteins and fats, is found in yeast, liver, meats, whole grain cereals, fish, and vegetables. Vitamin B_6 deficiency causes nerve inflammation, skin oiliness, and occasional convulsions in infants. The recommended adult dietary allowance of vitamin B_6 is 1-2 mg a day.

Vitamin B_{12} (cyanocobalamin) is required for the formation of red blood cells and for the proper functioning of nerves. It is found in liver, meats, and dairy products. Persons who cannot absorb vitamin B_{12} from the stomach develop a deficiency state called pernicious anemia that is treated by vitamin B_{12} injections, with dramatic relief of symptoms. Because vitamin B_{12} is not toxic, even in high doses, it has been used by doctors to treat fatigue of uncertain origin. Many tired middle-aged men and women come for their monthly injection of B_{12}, stating with certainty that they know, without referring to the calendar, when their 30 days are up. Although some ivory tower doctors scoff at this practice, family physicians who daily encounter fatigued patients find that injection of B_{12} is often a helpful form of therapy. The recommended adult dietary allowance for vitamin B_{12} is 1-3 micrograms per day.

Vitamin C (ascorbic acid) is important in forming connective tissue and promoting wound healing, and has been recommended to protect against the common cold. Scurvy, the legendary deficiency disease of sailors, results in loose teeth, inflamed gums, and hemorrhage under the skin. Vitamin C is found primarily in citrus fruits; in days gone by, English sailing ships prevented scurvy by introducing limes and lemons into the diet of their sailors. Consequently, the English sailors, to this day, are called Limeys. The recommended adult dietary allowance of vitamin C is 70-150 mg daily.

Vitamin D controls the metabolism of calcium and phosphorus of bone and is found in fish, liver, oils, eggs, milk, butter, and sunlight. Adults with vitamin D deficiency show a softening of the bones called osteomalacia, not unlike rickets in children. The recommended adult dietary allowance of vitamin D is 400 units per day.

Folic acid, active in the production of red blood cells, is found in green leafy vegetables and liver; a folic acid deficiency results in a particular type of anemia. The recommended daily adult dietary allowance of folic acid is 0.5-1 mg.

Pantothenic acid is important in the metabolism of fats, proteins, and carbohydrates. It is found in liver, egg yolk, and vegetables; a deficiency of pantothenic acid results in a failure to grow, in skin lesions, and in poor antibody formation. The recommended daily dietary allowance of pantothenic acid is 3-10 mg.

Vitamin K is important in blood clotting, and a deficiency may result in hemorrhage. The anticoagulants, often prescribed for the heart attack victim to "thin out the blood," act by neutralizing vitamin K. Bacteria within the intestine produce vitamin K from the constituents of a normal diet, and no definite dietary allowance has been established for this vitamin.

Vitamin E (tocopherol) plays an obscure metabolic role, and a deficiency of vitamin E may result in muscular degeneration. Vitamin E is found in vegetables, lettuce, eggs, and cereal products. No definite dietary allowance has been recommended, but vitamin E is a favorite of food faddists, who attribute to it a wide range of supposed therapeutic benefits. Vitamin E-containing skin preparations have broadened the horizons of this mysterious chemical compound.

IRON-DEFICIENCY ANEMIA

Iron-deficiency anemia is found in the older person who survives on a diet of milk, crackers, tea, and toast. "I couldn't chew meat even if I could afford it." Senior citizens need a daily portion of meat to maintain their bodies' iron content. Because the body absorbs only 5 to 10 per cent of the iron that is eaten each day, an older person consuming an iron-poor diet can gradually develop a very severe anemia.

The symptoms of iron-deficiency anemia are weakness, pallor, and breathlessness. The physician diagnoses iron-deficiency anemia when a test shows the hemoglobin to be below 9 or 10 grams. The doctor should perform a yearly hemoglobin test on all elderly persons whose diet is suspect. Iron-deficiency anemia responds promptly to the administration of iron tablets by mouth; with the multitude of inexpensive iron-containing vitamin preparations available today, iron-deficiency anemia should become a textbook curiosity in the United States.

OBESITY IS A DISEASE

In a comment to David B. Henderson in the lobby of the U. S. House of Representatives, Thomas B. Reed once remarked, "I'll own up to two hundred pounds, but no gentleman ever weighs over two hundred." That was three generations ago.

Obesity is a disease of epidemic proportions in America today, the end product of a life of self-indulgence in food and drink. Perhaps obesity gets its start in early childhood, when American mothers equate food with love. The American mother shows that she loves her child by feeding him more and more. "If you love Mommy, you'll finish all your dinner." The child shows his love for his mother by consuming the huge helpings of food that are offered. The connection between food and love is subconsciously carried into later life and shows itself as overeating when the individual feels frustrated or insecure.

The symptoms of overweight are the banana split for dessert, puffing after one flight of stairs, dresses with gussets, and last year's Easter suit that doesn't quite fit.

Obesity can be measured by comparing your height and weight to the height-weight chart compiled by the Metropolitan Life Insurance Company. Recently specialists in nutrition have classified obesity by caliper measurement of skin folds at the back of the arm and in other areas.

The treatment of obesity should begin with a trip to the doctor, armed with a firm resolve to take the necessary steps to correct the weight problem. Obesity is treated by consuming a diet calculated to provide less calories per day than the daily activities require, thereby burning up fat and glycogen for energy. In simple language, the treatment for obesity is to eat less food. After a careful physical examination, your doctor may prescribe a "diet pill" to curb the appetite, but the conscientious physician will not prescribe diuretics, thyroid extract, or digitalis unless a specific indication for their use exists.

There are presently a number of weight-reduction clinics across the country. They employ frequent ritual weighings, keeping their patients so busy taking pills that they have little time to eat, and relieve the overweight middle-aged housewife of more dollars than pounds. The older person who has a weight problem should shun weight-reduction clinics and place his trust in the family physician, who has a comprehensive knowledge of his overall health picture.

The following is a reducing diet that has helped many senior citizens in my practice. A safe rate of weight loss is two pounds each week. The diet has been planned to give protein, vitamins, and other necessary nutrients, yet avoid high calorie foods. Eat the indicated amounts daily, not more or less. *Do not eat between meals.*

REDUCING DIET

Daily Meal Pattern	Sample Menu

BREAKFAST

1/2 cup citrus fruit or juice	1/2 cup orange juice
1 egg, poached or scrambled	1 poached egg
1 slice of toast	1 slice of toast
1 pat butter	1 pat butter
Coffee or tea (no cream or sugar)	Black coffee

LUNCH

Lean meat, cheese or cottage cheese: 2 oz.	Luncheon meat, 2 slices
1 vegetable serving	1 raw carrot
1 fruit serving	Cantaloupe balls, 1/2 cup
1 glass skimmed milk	1 glass skimmed milk

DINNER

Lean meat, poultry, or fish: 4 oz.	Roast chicken, leg or breast
1 vegetable serving	String beans, 1/2 cup
1 salad serving	Tossed green salad, lemon juice dressing
Coffee or tea (no cream or sugar)	1 cup of tea

The following luxury foods must be avoided:

approx. calories

Milk shake	*400*
Pie or cake	*350*
Ice cream	*250*
Cocktail	*175*
Beer (8 oz.)	*110*
Soda (8 oz.)	*110*
Nuts (10)	*100*
Potato chips (10)	*100*

Staying slim requires day-to-day diet planning. Youthful follies of chocolate cake, ice cream, and candy are gone forever. While the older person may allow himself a rare treat, a weight problem can be avoided only by strict adherence to a diet of meat, fish, vegetables, fresh fruits, and some dairy products. Only constant vigilance can prevent obesity.

A
Sound
Mind

The fountain of contentment must spring up in the mind.

SAMUEL JOHNSON
(1709-1784)

THE NORMAL CHANGES OF AGING

Michel de Montaigne once observed that the mind grows constipated and sluggish as it grows old. Hardening of the arteries causes a diminished blood flow to the cells of the cerebrum, the site of conscious thought and volitional activity; the cerebellum, the control center for coordination and balance; and the brain stem, which governs breathing, blood pressure, and pulse rate and connects the spinal cord with higher centers (see Figure 1). With less oxygen to fuel metabolism and less nutrients available for repair, the brain cells are unable to operate at top efficiency; the consequent indolent mental function shows itself in subtle ways.

The decreased mental function that normally accompanies aging may begin in the 60's or 70's. Some lucky people will not experience the deterioration until their 80's, or later. The decrease in mental function, caused by hardening of the arteries to the brain, is often associated with arteriosclerosis in other parts of the body. Because diabetes, hypertension, obesity, and high blood cholesterol are causally

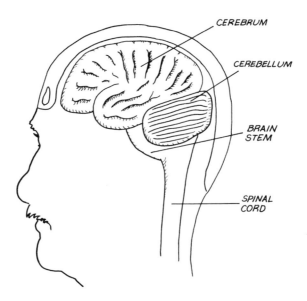

Fig. 1. The Brain and Spinal Cord

related to hardening of the arteries, these conditions often accompany mental slowdown in the later years.

A failure of memory for recent events heralds the mental changes of aging: the older person cannot bring to mind the name of a close friend, or remember what he had for breakfast, or recall the title of the movie he saw last night. Coupled with this failure of recent memory, there is often an improved memory for events that happened in the past, the individual recalling clearly an event that occurred 20 or even 40 years ago and relating details such as the exact time of day, the clothes worn, or the exact words spoken.

A failure of judgment, often imperceptible under ordinary circumstances, is a frequent second stage of mental slowdown after age 65. The older person offers snap opinions, lacking the careful study that he would have given the decision in prior years. There is a paucity of creative thought, coupled with an increased reliance upon opinions formed in the past.

Sometimes older persons will become cranky and will find fault easily. Nocturnal restlessness, a sleepless tendency to wander at night, can indicate senile brain disease. A previously fastidious person may become careless about personal cleanliness, and his dress may become sloppy and unkempt.

The treatment of the normal changes of aging should be a partnership between the patient, the family, and the physician. The keynote of treatment is Thoreau's advice to all who feel that the world moves too fast: Simplify, Simplify! The older person's toilet should be easily accessible from his bed, and there should be night lights to prevent nocturnal confusion. Because of the danger of wandering or accidental injury in the home, the oldster with marginal mental function should not be left alone for long periods of time. Persons whose judgment has been impaired must be protected from entering into business transactions without competent legal advice and guidance.

The physician will sometimes treat chronic brain slowdown with drugs called vasodilators, which help open the hardened arteries to the brain. Examples of vasodilators are papaverine, Arlidin, Hydergine, and Vasodilan; although their action is usually not dramatic, long-term effects have been beneficial in some patients.

ANXIETY

1793183

Anxiety occurs at all ages and is not solely a disease of persons over 65. About A.D. 1000, Ali ibn-Hazm wrote, "No one is moved to act, or resolves to speak a single word, who does not hope by means of this action or word to release anxiety from his spirit." Because older persons often lack the insight, resources, and stability to tolerate anxiety, the result can be an incapacitating state of near panic.

Anxiety is a frightful feeling of anticipation, usually with no specific cause, causing drenching sweats, dry mouth, pounding heartbeat, frightened eyes, and tremors of the hands and lips. The anxious patient appears fearful, but cannot pinpoint the cause of his apprehension.

In a sense, anxiety is an exaggeration of a normal reaction, caused by release of adrenalin into the bloodstream, such as would occur in a dangerous situation. If you have ever had a near accident in an automobile and remember the tense and shaking feeling that immediately followed the experience, you know how the anxious patient feels at all times. The treatment of chronic anxiety involves scrupulous attention to good health measures, since anxiety will often occur in persons whose health is impaired for other reasons. Regularity is reassuring. The anxious person must live a well-organized life with three balanced meals daily, eight hours of sleep a night, and an adequate balance of work and relaxation.

Many cases of anxiety occur as ambitious persons take on more responsibility than they are psychologically equipped to handle, while others can be traced to financial or family problems. The anxious

individual and his doctor must spend some time discussing the underlying causes of anxiety and take steps to minimize these factors. The
prescription of a mild tranquilizer such as Valium or Librium will be
helpful in reducing the patient's symptoms while he strives to reduce
tension in his daily life.

DEPRESSION

Depression is a distressing feeling of worthlessness. "Life just isn't
worth living any more." Many depressed persons have also experienced
pain and, if questioned, will state that they would much rather have
their pain than depression. Depression may follow an obvious cause;
indeed, the older person is especially vulnerable to such adverse conditions as a death in the family, the sale of a home, or the loss of some
cherished possession. Frequently, however, the depressed person has no
specific cause for his downcast feelings.

The symptoms of depression are decreased appetite, fatigue, and
frequent crying. A cardinal symptom of depression is awaking early in
the morning, unable to get back to sleep. The patient feels worthless
and dejected and sometimes entertains suicidal thoughts.

Despite the overwhelming symptoms, the forecast for the depressed patient is sunny. Depression, like the barometer, goes up and
down, and the patient may be assured that no matter how his disease is
treated, the clouds of depression will pass.

Depression should be treated by a psychotherapist or by a family
doctor with a special interest in emotional problems. The medical
treatment of depression includes antidepressants or psychic energizers
such as Elavil, Tofranil, or Navane.

PSYCHOSIS

Psychosis is a specific medical term describing a complete breakdown in
mental function. We will discuss the senile form of psychosis, once
called senile dementia, which represents an exaggeration of the normal
changes of aging.

Swift, in *Gulliver's Travels*, describes a being called the Struldbrug
—an immortal being. The newborn Strulbrug has a circular red spot on
the forehead over the left eyebrow, "which was an infallible mark that
it would never die." Although Struldbrugs could not physically die,
they were doomed to the progressive mental changes of advanced age.
Swift's description of these Struldbrugs parallels senile psychosis:

"When they [the Struldbrugs] came to four score years they were not only opinionated, peevish, covetous, morose, vain, talkative; but incapable of friendship and dead to all natural affection . . . envy and impotent desires are their prevailing passions . . . at 90 they lose their teeth and hair; they have, at that age, no distinction of taste, but eat and drink whatever they can without relish or appetite."

The senile psychotic patient may be withdrawn. His lack of memory may be balanced, so to speak, by confabulation, the imaginative manufacture of events to fill the gaps in memory. There may be confusion as to time, place, and person. Auditory or visual hallucinations—seeing God or talking to a long-deceased relative—are common, and there may be feelings of persecution, the belief that other family members are plotting against him. Some senile psychotic patients have "ideas of influence," a medical term meaning that the person thinks he can change the ebb and flow of the tides, the movement of the sun, or the growth of a flower.

Medical treatment of the senile psychotic patient is less hopeful than the therapy of the depressed individual. The patient with senile psychosis should be admitted to a mental hospital, sanitarium, or first-class nursing home, and psychotherapy should be made available within the limits of the patient's mental abilities.

Drug therapy will include tranquilizers, usually of the phenothiazine family: Thorazine, Mellaril, Sparine, and others. Most patients with senile psychosis are eventually admitted to institutions for permanent care.

The Aging Ear

Yet is was not possible for me to say to men:
Speak louder, shout, for I am deaf. Alas!
How could I declare the weakness of a sense
which in me ought to be more acute than in
others . . .

LUDWIG VAN BEETHOVEN

(1770-1827)

Letter to his brothers

October 6, 1802

PRESBYCUSIS

As the ear grows older, it is influenced by two of the general factors of aging: hardening of the arteries and stiffening of the joints. To understand the changes of aging, let us examine the function of the ear.

The ear is a fascinating device whereby sound waves in the air are received and transmitted to the brain for interpretation (see Figure 2).

The external ear is a trumpet designed to pick up sound waves and channel them into the ear canal. At the end of that canal, about three-quarters of an inch from the outside, is the eardrum, a very thin, almost transparent membrane closing the end of the ear canal and vibrating in response to sound waves. When the eardrum vibrates, it sets in motion three tiny bones that are joined, one to another: the familiar hammer, anvil, and stirrup that you studied in school days.

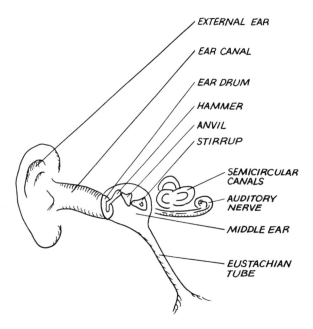

EXTERNAL EAR

EAR CANAL

EAR DRUM

HAMMER

ANVIL

STIRRUP

SEMICIRCULAR CANALS

AUDITORY NERVE

MIDDLE EAR

EUSTACHIAN TUBE

Fig. 2. The Ear

The hammer, anvil, and stirrup lie in the middle ear, an air-filled cavity behind the eardrum and connected to the throat by the eustachian tube. Sound waves are transmitted through the base of the stirrup into the inner ear. The base of the stirrup is oval in shape and fits into the so-called oval window in the temporal bone of the skull, which houses the inner ear. From here, the sound impulses are picked up by the auditory nerve, which carries them directly to the brain. Near the auditory nerve are found the semicircular canals, which control balance.

Presbycusis is a medical term for the progressive hearing loss that occurs with age. As the years roll on, hardening of the arteries reduces the blood flow to all areas of the ear, particularly the auditory nerve, resulting in a partial loss of hearing.

Hearing also suffers because of stiffness of the joints between the hammer, anvil, and stirrup. The base of the stirrup may stiffen in the oval window. When this occurs, there is a characteristic type of deafness that can be corrected by a highly effective operation called stapes mobilization that frees the base of the stirrup and restores normal vibration.

Sound waves occur at different frequencies. High-frequency waves cause high-pitched sounds such as a soprano voice, while low-frequency sound waves may be represented by a deep bass voice. The perception of high-frequency sound waves is more vulnerable to damage; the older man with hearing problems will characteristically have a high-frequency hearing defect, experiencing difficulty in hearing his wife's high voice, but having no trouble hearing the deeper voices of his cronies. The person with presbycusis will find that background noise increases his hearing problem.

Very loud noises, either a single explosion or persistent exposure to loud sounds, can cause a hearing defect that mimics presbycusis. Many teenagers with their rock music played at a decibel level approaching the pain threshold cause permanent damage to the hearing mechanism. It is as though the ear, sensing that repeated loud noises are potentially damaging to the mind and body, adjusts the volume by decreasing hearing acuity.

The older person with a hearing problem should seek the advice of his family physician. An audiogram, a simple hearing test that can be performed in the office, will show the extent and type of hearing loss. A look into the ears and a tuning-fork examination to test auditory nerve function will complete the procedure. Your doctor then will be able to tell you whether you should see an ear specialist for possible surgery, be fitted for a hearing aid, or have the ear wax removed.

But heed the words of Elizabeth Corbett in the October 1965 issue of the *Atlantic Monthly*: "A sudden improvement in hearing is not always an unmixed blessing, as many an older person living in a household full of noisy grandchildren has discovered."

EXTERNAL EAR INFECTION

External ear infection is a painful inflammation of the ear canal. There is loss of hearing, and pus may drain from the ear. This often follows the entry of foreign substances into the ear; swimming, with water driving bacteria into the ear canal under pressure, is a common means of acquiring such an infection. Cleaning the ears with cotton-tipped applicators inserted deep into the ear canal, scraping the tissues, and packing the wax, may well cause an ear canal infection.

The treatment of such an infection involves the frequent application of ear drops, sometimes applied to a cotton wick in the ear if the swelling is extreme. Various drops may be prescribed, including astringent solutions, antibiotics, and pain killers. Antibiotics may be taken by mouth if the infection is severe; the patient should not allow water or cotton-tipped applicators to enter the ear. Ear canal infections often respond slowly to therapy, and the sufferer should have patience with his doctor and the medication.

The patient who has suffered with ear canal infection in the past seems to be more prone to its occurrence in the future. Susceptible persons should retain the therapeutic ear drops prescribed by the doctor and, with his approval, introduce these into the ears at the first sign of recurrence.

MIDDLE EAR INFECTION

Middle ear infection is a bacterial inflammation of the middle ear cavity. Bacteria gain access via the eustachian tube. Middle ear infection in adults is often related to some change in the pressure surrounding the ears, such as swimming under water, mountain travel, or flying in unpressurized aircraft. The symptoms of middle ear infection are severe pain in the infected ear, a drop in hearing, and occasional episodes of dizziness. If the infection has built up sufficient pressure, the eardrum may burst, with blood and pus filling the ear canal.

Middle ear infection is treated with antibiotics to combat bacteria. Decongestants are indispensable in the treatment of such infection to reduce swelling in the eustachian tube and release pressure into the throat; nose drops sometimes help by opening the eustachian tube. Analgesic tablets such as aspirin, Darvon, or Zactirin may be necessary for pain, and the application of a heating pad or hot water bottle to the ear may reduce discomfort. If the eardrum has not burst, warm mineral oil or anesthetic drops such as Auralgan placed in the ear canal help relieve painful eardrum pressure.

Middle ear infection is prevented by avoiding sudden changes in pressure on the middle ear, particularly when a cold may cause partial blockage of the eustachian tube. The potential sources of sudden changes in ear pressure are flying in unpressurized aircraft, swimming, scuba diving, motoring over high mountains, and elevator rides in skyscrapers. When changing pressure is unavoidable, chewing gum with rhythmic swallowing helps relieve middle ear pressure.

LABYRINTHITIS

Labyrinthitis is an inflammation of the inner ear. The inner ear has two functions: the transmission of sound waves via the auditory nerve and the control of balance.

The balance mechanism is composed of three semicircular, fluid-filled canals set at right angles to one another. Upon movement of the head, the fluid in these canals is set in motion, and the motion of this fluid reflects the movement of the body. The brain then makes the necessary muscular adjustments to maintain balance.

Labyrinthitis is an inflammation of the inner ear that causes a particular type of dizziness called vertigo, a sensation of whirling. The patient may feel the room spinning about him or have a feeling that the room is stationary and he is revolving like a top. Most labyrinthitis is caused by viruses, and the course is self-limited, although full recovery may take as long as eight weeks. During that time the patient may be subject to periodic recurrence of symptoms.

The treatment of viral labyrinthitis is by antihistamines such as Dramamine or Bonine to reduce the symptoms of vertigo. Because vertigo is accentuated by rapid movements of the ear, the patient should move slowly when changing his position: standing up, rolling over, or turning the head. Since vertigo is a frightening symptom, the patient should seek medical attention for diagnosis and reassurance.

MÉNIÈRE'S DISEASE

Ménière's disease is an inflammation of the inner ear characterized by three symptoms: ringing or buzzing in the ear, impaired hearing, and vertigo. The exact cause of Ménière's disease is an enigma, but it seems to be related to an excess of fluid in the semicircular canals of the inner ear. It is most common in middle-aged women, but symptoms may persist into the later years, and some cases will begin after age 65. Patients note a persistent buzzing or ringing noise in one or both ears, with hearing loss in at least one ear. Sufferers from Ménière's disease will have recurrent episodes of whirling or vertigo similar to those found in labyrinthitis.

The disease is treated with a variety of medications, which indicates that none is spectacularly successful. Because of the prevailing theory that Ménière's disease is related to excessive fluid in the semicircular canals in the middle ear, diuretics (water pills) are often prescribed. Antihistamines such as those used in labyrinthitis are often recommended, and vasodilators—medication to improve blood flow in peripheral arteries—have been used in selected cases. With advancing age, the disease comes to be less of a problem to the patient; if sufficient time is allowed, many sufferers find that their symptoms, like old soldiers, fade away.

The Aging Eye

PRESBYOPIA

While several eye diseases are found almost exclusively in older persons, the eye changes that are the direct result of aging are termed presbyopia. To understand presbyopia, let us consider the function of the eye.

The eye is a camera; light that enters through the pupil is bent by the cornea and lens, and the image is focused on the retina of the back of the eye (see Figure 3). When at rest, the eye is perfectly accommodated to distance vision. However, when reading or doing close work, the tiny eye muscles behind the iris act on the lens to make it thicker to increase the bending of light rays. The normal lens has an elasticity that allows it to be bent to accommodate to close vision.

With increasing age, the lens loses its elasticity and assumes a resting state, well accommodated to distance vision, but unable to be thickened to adjust to close work. This loss of elasticity of the lens and progressive loss of ability to accommodate for near work is called presbyopia.

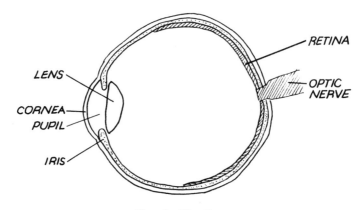

Fig. 3. The Eye

DO I NEED GLASSES?

Glasses, or corrective lenses as they are properly called, allow the eye to adjust to an imperfection in the lens or cornea. In the normal eye the cornea and the lens both bend light rays to focus the image on the retina. Some eyes focus the rays too far in front of the retina and some eyes focus the rays behind it. These eyes will need corrective lenses to adjust the proper focus of the light image.

Nearsightedness (myopia) is characterized by an excessive bending of the light rays, probably caused by an abnormally curved cornea or by a lens that is too thick. The nearsighted eye focuses the light rays in front of the retina, and the brain cells receive a distorted image. Nearsightedness is corrected by eyeglasses to reduce the bending of light rays and focus the light image directly on the retina.

In farsightedness (hyperopia), the light rays are improperly bent, focusing the image behind the retina. The eye with presbyopia is farsighted, the lens fails to thicken to accommodate to close work, and the retina receives a distorted image, which is passed on to the brain. The treatment for farsightedness is the prescription of corrective lenses to focus the light rays farther forward in the eye.

Astigmatism is a defect in vision caused by an irregular curve of the cornea, the outer layer of the eye. The cornea, like the lens of the eye, bends the light rays, helping to form a sharp image on the retina. Irregularities of the cornea cause the retina to receive a distorted image. Astigmatism is a disease of all ages and is treated by corrective lenses to compensate for the effect of corneal irregularity.

Abnormalities of vision can cause headache, fatigue, and red eyes. The farsighted eye will cause more such symptoms than the nearsighted eye, because in farsightedness the muscles holding the lens are called into action almost constantly to bend light rays entering the eye.

Abnormal vision can be caused by factors other than a distorted cornea or lens. Some of the tranquilizers or antihypertensive drugs can disturb the eye's ability to accommodate to near vision. Diabetes mellitus, especially when out of control or coming under control, may cause disturbing visual changes. Abnormalities of vision are one of the first signs of toxicity caused by sulfa drugs. Cataracts and other diseases of the eye, which will be discussed in this chapter, are common causes of visual changes.

CONJUNCTIVITIS

Conjunctivitis is an inflammation of the outer layers of the eye, causing an irritated, itching, burning sensation, mimicking a speck of dust in the eye. A common condition, conjunctivitis is often seen when the person is run-down for other reasons such as a cold or viral influenza.

Often caused by viruses, the common pinkeye is a highly contagious disease. A bacterial conjunctivitis will show pus running from both eyes; while it is apparently a more severe disease than viral pinkeye, it responds more readily to treatment.

Conjunctivitis is treated with antibiotic eyedrops or ointment. Because ointment blurs the vision, older persons usually prefer to use eyedrops. Since tears bathe the eye constantly and rapidly wash out all foreign substances, eyedrops must be administered at intervals of one or two hours. Almost all commonly used antibiotics have been employed to treat conjunctivitis. Chloramphenicol eyedrops are potent and safe for use in the eye; neomycin, bacitracin, and Polymyxin are common constituents of eye preparations, while other eyedrops include sulfonamides and the mycin drugs. Viral or bacterial conjunctivitis will usually respond to therapy within three to four days.

Since many acute inflammations of the eye will first be noticed as redness of the eye, it is important to note that conjunctivitis does not cause acute pain or a decrease in vision. Some tearing of the eye may cause transient blurring of vision, or there may be an itching burning discomfort; however, severe sharp pain, a noticeable decrease in vision, or a failure of the eye to respond to eyedrops within a three-day period should prompt a visit to your doctor.

IRITIS

Iritis is an inflammation of the deeper tissues of the eye. It is similar to conjunctivitis in that it represents an inflammation of the lining tissues of the eye and presents itself as redness, but it is a more serious condition and a threat to vision. The patient with iritis will notice a definite pain and a decrease in vision in the involved eye, perhaps associated with a sensation of tiny spots floating in the eye.

Iritis may be a viral or bacterial infection, a response to injury to the eye, or have an unknown cause.

The treatment of iritis belongs in the hands of an eye specialist, who will usually prescribe eyedrops to relax the muscles that normally are used to thicken the lens, to "put the eye to rest" for the duration of the disease. He may also prescribe cortisone, antibiotics, or other medication. The duration of iritis is highly variable, lasting weeks, months, or sometimes years.

SPOTS BEFORE THE EYES

"Floaters" are small moving specks in the field of vision, occurring at all ages, but more common after age 65. Almost all floaters are crystals that have formed in the thick fluid, the vitreous humor, of the eye. Although these floaters are a nuisance, they are harmless, and there is no treatment available.

Infrequently, floaters may be the first sign of severe eye disease, notably retinal detachment, a condition in which the retina tears away from the back wall of the eye. Retinal detachment is curable by surgery if detected early, but if neglected and allowed to progress it can cause permanent blindness.

A sudden shower of floaters in an eye which was previously normal is cause for an examination by the doctor. If the retinal tear is undetected, there will then follow a loss of vision in part of the retina, with a corresponding blind spot in the field of vision. This second warning should prompt an immediate examination for anyone experiencing these symptoms. The final stage, as the retina tears away from the back of the eye, is a sudden loss of vision sometimes likened to pulling down a window shade. Prompt therapy is essential to save the vision in the affected eye.

CATARACT

Cataract is the best known of the degenerative eye diseases. The lens of the eye becomes cloudy, and the light rays cannot pass through to the normal retina beyond.

Cataracts show a definite family tendency and are quite common in diabetics. The physician will diagnose a cataract by examination of the eye with an ophthalmoscope, an instrument for viewing the interior of the eye. If a cataract is present, the doctor will be unable to view the retina of the eye because of the cloudy lens behind the pupil. If the patient cannot see out through the lens, the doctor cannot see in.

The treatment for cataract is surgical removal of the cloudy lens and the prescription of thick glasses to accommodate for the absent lens. The operation is almost uniformly successful.

The most important aspect of cataract surgery is proper timing of the operation. Cataracts grow at a highly variable rate. The cataract is said to be "mature" and ready for surgery when the patient is unable to use his eyes to perform his usual activities. Consequently, librarians or watchmakers will find that their cataracts mature before the farmer, who does not use his eyes for close work. In the average patient, I advise that their cataracts are ready for surgery when they can no longer read the daily newspaper.

GLAUCOMA

Glaucoma sneaks in like a thief in the night, robbing the unwary patient of his vision. An elevation of the pressure of fluid within the eye, glaucoma has begun in 2 per cent of persons over age 40. It has been estimated that there are up to one million cases of undiscovered glaucoma in the United States today. Surveys have shown that 10 to 12 per cent of all blindness in this country is caused by this disease.

The eye is a sac filled with fluid. The fluid within the eye is formed constantly, and the overflow exits from the eye through small ducts. In glaucoma, the fluid continues to form at the normal rate, but the drainage ducts become blocked, and pressure within the eye mounts. The blockage of the ducts occurs slowly, and there may be no symptoms. Both eyes are usually affected. Glaucoma may be painless or may cause a constant aching of the eyes. Glaucoma can steal the last speck of vision without ever causing telltale pain in the eyes.

Glaucoma is detected by a measurement of the fluid pressure of the eye, a painless examination performed with an instrument called a tonometer. The physician instills in the eye a drop or two of a local anesthetic that will not interfere with vision. The anesthetic numbs the eye; with the patient reclining, the tonometer is placed on the eye to measure the pressure (see Figure 4). The normal pressure of the eye should be below 18 to 20 mm of mercury; if the pressure is found to be higher, glaucoma is probably the culprit.

The treatment of glaucoma is the instillation of eyedrops such as pilocarpine to help unplug the ducts that carry excess fluid from the eye. Although surgery is sometimes necessary, most cases can be well controlled by the regular use of the eyedrops.

Can glaucoma be prevented? Probably not. However, because the disease is related to increased fluid pressure in the eye, it may be wise to cut the consumption of salt after your fortieth birthday.

Because glaucoma can progress to severe visual impairment with almost no symptoms, it is imperative that every person over 65 have an annual eye examination.

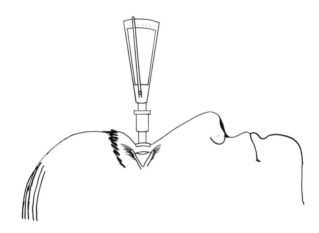

Fig. 4. Tonometer Test for Glaucoma

The Nose
and Throat
After 65

Sit down now and pray forsooth that the
mucus in your nose may not run! Nay,
rather wipe your nose and do not blame God.
EPICTETUS
(Ca. A.D. 90)

THE CHANGES OF AGING

The nose and throat, shown in Figure 5, are the portals through which life-sustaining air and food enter the body. With age, the mucus glands, whose duty it is to keep the membranes moist and help moisten the air going to the lungs, begin to dry out. The hair within the nose, which filters the air flowing to the lungs, becomes sparse, and foreign particles slip through into the bronchial tubes. The membranes of the nose and throat undergo the degenerative processes of aging and become more susceptible to irritation and infection. Thin tissues of the nose may bleed more easily, and dry irritated sinus membranes are easy targets for infection. A lifetime of smoking or exposure to air pollution can lead to chronic sore throat, hoarseness, or recurrent infections and may progress to cancer of the throat or larynx.

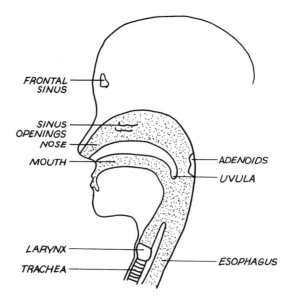

FRONTAL SINUS

SINUS OPENINGS

NOSE

MOUTH

ADENOIDS

UVULA

LARYNX

TRACHEA

ESOPHAGUS

Fig. 5. The Nose and Throat

THE COMMON COLD

The common cold is the curse of winter, causing an uncomfortable congestion in the head, loss of appetite, pressure on the ears, a mild sore throat, tickle in the throat, and cough. Persons over 65 are much more vulnerable to secondary complications than younger people. More than a hundred different species of viruses cause symptoms of the common cold; because so many different organisms are involved, it has been difficult to prepare a truly effective vaccine against it.

How to treat the common cold? Sir Alexander Fleming, the discoverer of penicillin suggested, "A good gulp of hot whiskey at bedtime—it's not very scientific, but it helps."

Medically, treatment of the common cold includes the use of decongestants to reduce swelling of inflamed membranes; pseudo-ephedrine is a widely used product. Antihistamines are often prescribed as drying agents when excessive mucus forms. In the past, atropine derivatives were used as drying agents for the common cold, but their use in the elderly can lead to constipation and flare-ups of glaucoma. Cough medicines containing dextromethorphan or possibly codeine will be prescribed if cough is severe. Nose drops such as one-quarter per cent Neo-Synephrine help relieve nasal congestion; if fever occurs, antibiotics are often prescribed for the treatment of secondary complications. Bed rest, adequate fluids, and fruit juices for their vitamin C content are also prescribed. Aspirin remains our best drug for the aches and pains of the common cold.

Some colds may be prevented by following these rules:
Avoid crowds during the winter.
Don't visit friends with colds.
Get plenty of rest.
Take vitamin C in fruit juice daily.
Avoid unnecessary exposure to cold weather.

SINUS TROUBLE

"Sinus trouble" is a catchall term that includes nasal allergy, chronic postnasal drip, sniffling caused by house dust, animal dander, or pollen, and true sinus infection. The typical patient resides in a humid area, often a river valley or coastal region; long-term residents of the Hudson Valley in New York State can gab for hours, comparing their symptoms of so-called sinus trouble, which causes chronic nasal congestion, catarrh, and periodic blowing of the nose like a foghorn on a stormy night.

The observant patient may find that his symptoms are worse at a certain time of the year, such as June or September; in that case, his sinus trouble is really an allergy to grass, tree, or ragweed pollen. Some patients, upon careful questioning, will discover that their sinus trouble is noted only in the house, in the workshop, or in the barn, and these patients may be allergic to house dust, sawdust, or molds. Other individuals will notice that their sinus trouble is worse when the weather is damp, while still other sufferers will have a prolonged flare-up each time a common cold occurs.

The treatment of such trouble is really the treatment of the underlying condition. Those with an allergy are treated with antihistamines and possibly desensitization injections. Sufferers whose disease is related to change in atmospheric conditions should consult their physician concerning the possible benefits of air conditioning, humidification, and air filtration. Those with true chronic sinus infection should receive adequate therapy with antibiotics, decongestants, nose drops and, in some cases, enzymes to dissolve the thick sticky mucus in the sinus cavities.

ALLERGY

Allergy, a problem at all ages, can strike the senior citizen, and allergic symptoms superimposed upon possible chronic bronchitis, emphysema, or congestive heart failure can represent a severe threat to health. Although there may be sensitivity to food, medication, or plants, the most common allergic symptoms are noted in the nose, throat, and chest. Sneezing is the hallmark of the allergic patient, and the extended forefinger passing under the itching nose has been called the allergic salute. The allergy sufferer will show chronic nasal congestion and red itching eyes.

The treatment of allergy includes medication to relieve the symptoms and desensitization injections to reduce the sufferer's sensitivity to the product causing the allergy. Most allergy sufferers will benefit from antihistamines; in more severe cases, cortisone is sometimes used for short periods. Air conditioning with filtration of the air is of tremendous benefit to allergy sufferers, and the allergy victim should inspect his home carefully for possible reservoirs of house dust. It may be necessary to replace carpets with tile and draperies with pull shades and install muslin covers over air vents to filter out small dust particles. Dogs and cats should be banished from the home, and cigarette smoking should not be allowed in the house.

If these measures fail to give satisfactory relief and if the symptoms are severe, the older person should be referred to an allergy specialist for skin testing to discover the exact substances causing the allergy. Following determination of the causative factors, the allergist may prepare a vaccine to be administered by injection at regular, but progressively longer, intervals to desensitize the person to the offending substances.

NOSEBLEED

Many nosebleeds will occur with a common cold, the bleeding coming from a small area just inside and toward the middle of the nose (see Figure 6). Simple nosebleeds will respond to sustained pressure on the nose with a clean handkerchief; a nosebleed that does not stop within a short period of time should be brought to the attention of the physician for evaluation and treatment.

Nosebleed in the elderly can be the first sign of a more serious illness. If the blood pressure is elevated, the arteries will relieve the pressure through the weakest point in the system. Often the release

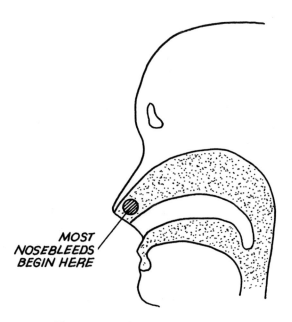

Fig. 6. Usual Site of Nosebleed

valve is through the nose, with heavy nosebleed signaling the presence of high blood pressure. Nosebleed may also be the first sign of a severe illness that has interfered with the formation of blood cells or impaired normal blood clotting. Leukemia and multiple myeloma may first be detected in apparently healthy persons who experience severe nosebleeds that have no obvious cause.

SORE THROAT

Sore throat, common at all ages, may be safely treated with warm salt water gargles and throat lozenges if mild and not accompanied by fever. The persistence of a sore throat for more than two days or the presence of a fever should prompt a call to the family physician.

The doctor will examine the throat and take a throat culture to determine the possible presence of streptococcus bacteria. Streptococcus causes a particularly troublesome throat infection that requires ten days of antibiotic treatment. The throat culture can be read in 18 to 24 hours by the doctor or his nurse, identifying the causative germ. After examination, the physician will determine the need for antibiotic therapy, antihistamines, or throat lozenges. Most sore throats respond to therapy within two or three days.

HOARSENESS

Hoarseness is a rasping speech that usually indicates simple laryngitis, but may occasionally be an early sign of more severe disease. Hoarseness of two or three days' duration accompanied by a mild feeling of malaise and possible fever may almost always be attributed to a viral laryngitis. There may be a mild sore throat and an aching in the joints. Laryngitis of this type may be safely treated with warm salt water gargles, throat lozenges, and antihistamines, but fever or failure to respond to therapy should prompt a visit to the doctor for accurate diagnosis.

Chronic hoarseness, the persistence of rasping speech for more than two or three weeks, calls for prompt medical investigation. Many cases of chronic hoarseness are caused by vocal nodules, small harmless growths on the vocal cords that can be detected by examination of the larynx with a mirror. Vocal nodules can be removed surgically by a throat specialist with good results and cessation of hoarseness. Chronic hoarseness, however, may be an early sign of cancer of the larynx and for this reason should not be tolerated for more than two or three weeks before being investigated by the doctor.

FLU

Flu or grippe, as it was once called, seems a serious threat to all persons over 65 who can recall the millions of flu deaths in 1918. The symptoms of flu include fever, headache, and aching joints, with loss of appetite and severe malaise. The flu victim feels too tired to roll over in bed. Although there may be a mild sore throat and cough, the patient lacks the usual symptoms of the common cold. Highly contagious, flu can spread through a nursing home like fleas in a pet shop.

The influenza virus is in a constant state of change, with new types evolving each year. As we develop immunity to type A or type B or the Hong Kong virus, a new strain to which we are not immune emerges in Taiwan or England or some other area. Upon isolation of such a new virus, the United States Public Health Service and the cooperating commercial laboratories will rush preparation of a flu vaccine to be used for prevention. In my opinion, the annual and frequently inaccurate prediction by the United States Public Health Service as to whether flu will be a problem each winter should not influence the senior citizen's decision concerning flu shots. All persons over the age of 65 are urged to take the flu shots each fall.

The treatment for flu includes bed rest, aspirin for fever, and fluids. For those persons who are nauseated or who cannot take aspirin, acetominophen is just as effective, but spares the stomach upset. Specific symptoms such as severe headache may be treated with stronger analgesics such as Darvon; throat lozenges are useful for mild sore throat; and expectorants are prescribed for cough. If the temperature soars above 103 degrees, the flu victim should be examined at home by the family doctor, who will decide whether antibiotics are needed.

Persons over 65 are easy prey for complications such as bronchitis and pneumonia. Any person with the flu whose condition seems to be deteriorating should be reexamined by his physician and hospitalization considered.

Some cases of flu can be prevented:

Avoid persons with the disease. Stay away from crowds during the flu season.

Maintain good general health with exercise, proper diet, and plenty of rest.

Flu shots are recommended for all senior citizens, especially those suffering from chronic disease.

CANCER OF THE THROAT

Cancer of the throat, a destructive tumor that grows fairly rapidly, is usually related to the curse of tobacco in pipes, cigars, or cigarettes. Cancer of the throat can usually be detected by examination through the mouth, and a careful inspection of the mouth and throat should be part of your annual physical examination.

Any white patches or persistent soreness in the throat should be brought to the attention of the physician; painful areas that are not reached by direct vision will be viewed by mirror examination. Suspicious sores will be referred to an oral surgeon for removal.

Cancer of the throat is curable by surgery if detected early in the disease but, if overlooked, it becomes progressively destructive. Advanced throat cancer is attacked by a combination of surgery and radiation therapy, but with only fair results.

CANCER OF THE LARYNX

The larynx or voice box is a fairly common site of cancer, usually occurring on the vocal cords. Early symptoms of cancer of the larynx are persistent hoarseness and local pain. Cancer of the larynx, if detected early by mirror examination or by direct vision with the laryngoscope, is completely curable by surgery. Advanced cancer of the larynx is treated by surgery or X ray, with variable results.

Removal of cancer of the larynx sacrifices the vocal cords. The person who has had a laryngectomy will, at least temporarily, breathe through a tube in his throat and must learn to talk again, using the muscles of the throat and tongue. Special lessons teach the laryngectomy patient to swallow air into the stomach and then belch it up through the throat, forming words as the air passes through the throat and by the tongue. With practice, and perhaps aided by an electronic amplifier, remarkably effective speech can be produced in this manner.

Cancer of the larynx seems to be related to the excessive use of cigarettes. Prevention of cancer of the larynx is in great measure dependent upon cessation of smoking.

The Mouth
and Teeth
After 65

Mouth: In man, the gateway to the soul; in woman, the outlet of the heart.
AMBROSE BIERCE
(1842-1914)

THE CHANGES OF AGING

A healthy mouth requires constant vigilance. With strict adherence to common sense rules of oral hygiene, many persons reach 65 with a reasonably intact set of teeth. The preparation for a healthy mouth in later years begins in childhood. Both children and persons over 65 must resist the temptation to indulge in sweets. The teeth should be brushed two or three times daily after eating, and the dentist should be visited twice yearly for cleaning, examination, and needed repair work.

As we grow older, the teeth wear unevenly, forming valleys and ridges in which food can accumulate; dental caries thus are a frequent problem in persons over 65. As occlusal surfaces grind down, irregularities of bite may loosen teeth in their sockets; this condition can be corrected by the dentist. Regular care, brushing after meals, and proper diet will help to prevent disease of the teeth and mouth.

59

TOOTHACHE

Toothache warns that the tooth is in danger. The normal tooth consists of enamel, the hardest substance in the body; dentin, a softer protein-calcium mixture; and pulp, which contains the nerve (see Figure 7). The nerve of the tooth reacts to heat, cold, and infection; dentists warn that recurrent drinking of very hot or very cold beverages can cause a chronic inflammation of the tooth that may lead to actual disease of the nerve.

Most toothaches, however, occur as a result of dental caries, cavities in the teeth caused by bacteria and decay. As the cavity tunnels into the enamel, hot and cold beverages threaten the nerve of the tooth, which sends off warning signals of pain. Toothaches may be temporarily relieved by local anesthetics such as Benzodent or Xylocaine Viscous, and pain killers such as aspirin, Darvon, or Zactirin. However, all cases of toothache should be examined by the dentist for correction of the underlying problem.

GUM DISEASE

Gum disease, also called periodontitis or pyorrhea, is an inflammation of the gums. The gums help to hold the teeth in their jaw sockets. Disease of the gums presents a serious problem to the older person because untreated gum disease can result in loss of all the teeth.

The symptoms are pain and bleeding, often with pus pockets at the gum line. Chewing may be uncomfortable, and small particles of

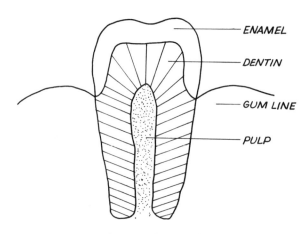

Fig. 7. The Tooth

food are found trapped in the gums near the teeth. Later in the disease, individual teeth may become loose.

Gum disease occurs as teeth wear unevenly and as abnormalities of bite place more pressure on one tooth than on others, loosening individual teeth in their sockets. Sometimes there are untreated dental caries in persons over 65 who eat too many refined carbohydrates. With sweets, dental caries, and teeth that are loose in their sockets, infection forms in the gums, quickly spreading to nearby tooth sockets and soon involving all gum surfaces.

The treatment of gum disease should be directed by the dentist, perhaps a periodontist, a specialist in disease of the gums. Antibiotics may be prescribed for infection, dental caries will be repaired, and sweets will be strictly forbidden. A program of regular brushing and gum massage will be instituted. Abnormalities of bite can be corrected by grinding down the appropriate surfaces of the teeth. I have found a preparation called Amosan helpful in very mild cases of gum diseases, but severe cases may require surgery. Failure of treatment of gum disease will result in a toothless grin, requiring a bridge or dentures.

Many cases of gum disease can be prevented:

Brush the teeth properly twice daily.

Avoid sweets.

Massage the gums each time the teeth are brushed.

Have a dental checkup twice yearly.

BAD BREATH

Bad breath, the elusive target of mouthwash commercials, besides being a social handicap, may be a warning of infection, nasal polyp, or simply trapped food particles. Bad breath is not a specific disease, but a symptom of many conditions; the treatment of bad breath will be the treatment of the underlying illness.

Chronic mouth breathing, caused by blockage of the nose, is a common cause of bad breath. The mouth breathing causes drying of normal saliva and allows entrance into the mouth of troublesome bacteria. Low-grade bacterial infection of the gums, the floor of the mouth, and the throat produces the foul odor of the breath. Treatment of this condition requires relieving the nasal obstruction, which may be caused by allergy or an enlarged nasal septum. When free breathing through the nose has been restored, the infection in the gums, mouth, and throat should be treated with appropriate antibiotics and rinses.

Since gum disease and decaying teeth may be the cause, all persons suspecting bad breath should be carefully examined by the dentist. In such cases, treatment of the underlying dental condition will relieve the bad breath problem.

A cleft tongue, a pocket across the back of the tongue, can collect food particles that disintegrate, causing a bad odor. Periodic cleansing of the pocket will remove the debris and, with it, the offensive odor.

Infection of the nasal cavity may be a cause of bad breath. Chronic low-grade bacterial infection of the nose and upper throat—the nasopharynx—can cause an offensive odor of the breath; infection of this type is treated with appropriate antibiotic therapy. I have found Furacin nasal solution, perhaps supplemented by antibiotic tablets or capsules, particularly effective.

Other causes of bad breath include chronic bronchitis, lung abscess, sinus infection, postnasal drip, and an infected nasal polyp. The treatment of bad breath in all cases depends upon the discovery of the causative factor and appropriate treatment of the underlying illness.

SORE TONGUE

Sore tongue, or glossitis, may be caused by a variety of factors; like bad breath, the therapy is dependent upon correct treatment of the cause. Common offenders are hot foods, tobacco, alcohol, and spices. Many victims of sore tongue are habitual pipe smokers who, drawing on their pipestems, subject the tongue to burn.

Sore tongue can arise from allergic reactions, perhaps to various components of toothpaste and mouthwashes or to certain dyes in food and candy.

Vitamin deficiency—particularly of the B vitamin group, as in pellagra—will cause a sore tongue, which responds dramatically to vitamin therapy.

A sore tongue may be a prominent sign of anemia. Pernicious anemia, a deficiency of vitamin B_{12}, will exhibit a sore tongue as a chief symptom, and iron-deficiency anemia may also cause a painful glossitis.

Moniliasis, a troublesome yeast infection, will cause a sore tongue, with white patches evident on the tongue, gums, and roof of the mouth. Common in diabetics and in persons taking large doses of antibiotics for long periods of time, the condition is also called thrush. The treatment for monilial infection of the mouth is local application of Mycostatin oral suspension four times daily, plus discontinuance of antibiotics.

CANKER SORES

Canker sores have been known since the time of Hippocrates. In most people, canker sores occur infrequently and are at worst a temporary nuisance, but in some elderly persons canker sores can be severe and almost disabling.

Canker sores are noted as small red areas within the mouth that soon break down to form a gray-white membrane. They are extremely painful, out of all proportion to the size of the sore. The cause of canker sores is not known, although citrus fruits, chocolate, menstrual periods, and viral infections have all been suspected.

The treatment of canker sores, whether mild and infrequent or severe and incapacitating, offers a sizable array of possibilities, none of which is particularly successful. In my experience, the most effective remedy for canker sores is local cauterization with silver nitrate in the doctor's office. This procedure is safe and almost painless. Occasionally a second cauterization is needed for stubborn lesions, but most disappear within a few days following this procedure.

Other agents for treatment have been trichloracetic acid, antibiotics, and various mouthwashes. There seems to be no foolproof method of preventing the recurrence of canker sores.

SALIVARY GLAND INFECTION

There are three pairs of salivary glands. Two sets lie under the tongue and jaw while the larger parotid glands are found in front of the ears. Disease may occur in any of the six glands; we are all familiar with mumps—a common childhood disease of the salivary glands.

Older persons may have stones or infection in their salivary glands. Here stones form when small bits of saliva crystallize; the small crystal will attract other particles of saliva and grow like a snowball to form a stone composed of calcium and phosphorus. The stone may pass spontaneously into the mouth or obstruct the duct between the salivary gland and the mouth, causing pain and enlargement of the blocked gland.

Removal of the stone from the gland is a task for the oral surgeon, who will use a small probe to coax the tiny stone along the duct. If neglected, the blocked salivary gland may develop infection, which will clear upon administration of appropriate antibiotics and removal of the stone.

Such infection may occur in the absence of stones in persons debilitated from other disease. Chronically ill persons in nursing homes often develop such severe infections, with a clinical picture not unlike mumps: fever, difficult swallowing, and severe pain and swelling in the salivary gland. Infections of this type are caused by bacteria and should be treated with local applications of heat to the salivary gland and large doses of the appropriate antibiotic: penicillin, erythromycin, or one of the new synthetic antibiotics.

Salivary gland infections found in disabled, debilitated elderly persons are a grave sign. The patient's weakened condition allows very little reserve to fight infection, and the condition is often the prelude to pneumonia, bloodstream infection, or a more serious terminal problem.

CANCER OF THE LIP AND TONGUE

Cancer of the lip and tongue will be considered together because of their close physical proximity, similar modes of treatment, and similar origin. Both are caused by long-term indulgence in pipe and cigar smoking. How right Philip Freneau was when he wrote two centuries ago, "Tobacco surely was designed, To poison, and destroy mankind." Cancer of the lip commonly strikes smokers who nurse hot pipestems, while cancer of the tongue is also prevalent in cigar smokers. The presence of a nagging sore on the tongue or lip should provoke prompt examination by the family physician, and all suspicious lesions should be removed immediately for diagnosis.

The initial attack on cancer of the lip and tongue is surgery. X-ray treatment is reserved for the more advanced cases that are not amenable to excision. Because of the easy accessibility for examination, cancer of the lip and tongue should be diagnosed early, and the outlook should be good.

Because of the relationship of cancer of the tongue and lip to smoking cigars and pipes, staying alive after 65 may be dependent on abandoning the habit.

The Senior Citizen and His Stomach

The members of the Body rebelled against the Belly, and said, "Why should we be perpetually engaged in administering to your wants, while you do nothing but take your rest, and enjoy yourself in luxury and self-indulgence?"

The members carried out their resolve, and refused their assistance to the Belly. The whole Body quickly became debilitated, and the hands, feet, mouth, and eyes, when too late, repented of their folly.

Aesop's Fables

THE CHANGES OF AGING

As we grow older, the stomach becomes critical and rebellious. The aging stomach grows intolerant of hot sausage, strong coffee, and pepperoni pizza as decreased gastric secretions cause the delicate cells of the stomach wall to rebel against spicy food. There may be some shrinkage of the volume of the stomach, so that large helpings cannot be tolerated, and frequent small feedings are needed. Since the aging stomach will complain about coarse food, a blender may be needed to assure the proper consistency. Weakness of the muscular wall of the stomach may prevent the smooth passage of food into the small intestine.

Almost all persons over 65 have found certain foods that their stomachs cannot tolerate; this group of troublesome foods should be scrupulously avoided to prevent indigestion.

DYSPEPSIA

"Doctor, everything I eat turns to acid in my stomach." Dyspepsia means faulty digestion of food, with a gnawing sensation in the upper abdomen, flatulence, nausea, and often heartburn caused by backwash of food and acid into the lower esophagus. Most persons with dyspepsia suffer if they eat certain types of food: coffee, the most common offender, stimulates the formation of large amounts of acid in the stomach. Cola drinks and tea also create acid, and spicy foods such as onions, garlic, hot sausage, hot peppers, pepperoni, and tomato sauce are frequent causes of dyspepsia.

Excessive stomach acid burns and irritates the stomach wall; if allowed to go untreated, the acorn of dyspepsia may grow into a great oak—peptic ulcer.

The treatment of dyspepsia aims to neutralize stomach acid and reduce further secretion. Antacids such as Maalox or Mylanta are prescribed at regular intervals, as is such antispasmodic medication as belladonna, Pro-Banthine, or Bentyl.

The cornerstone of the treatment of dyspepsia is the bland diet, eliminating spicy foods and offering nonirritating, soothing nutrients. The following is a bland diet that I have used successfully in my practice for some years.

BLAND DIET

Foods Allowed	Foods to Be Avoided
BREADS	
White bread, rolls, soda crackers	Bran and whole wheat breads and rolls
FRUITS	
Canned or stewed apple, prunes, apricot, peaches, and pears	All other canned or stewed fruit
	Raw fruits, except ripe banana
Dilute orange juice	
Ripe banana	
SOUPS	
Cream soups flavored with such vegetables as listed directly below	Lentil, bean, split pea, and meat-stock soups

VEGETABLES

Squash, lettuce, asparagus tips, carrots, lima beans, beets, spinach, peas, and string beans

Baked, mashed, or creamed white potatoes

All raw vegetables

Dried beans, peas, and lentils.

Brussels sprouts, cabbage, onion, broccoli, cauliflower, radishes, turnips, and tomato

CEREALS

Cooked oatmeal, Cream of Wheat, Farina, cornmeal and Wheatena

Bran and whole wheat cereals

MEATS, POULTRY, FISH, EGGS, AND CHEESE

White meat of chicken or turkey

Baked or steamed fresh fish

Broiled lamb, veal, or beef

Soft cooked eggs

Cottage or cream cheese

Pork, mutton, duck, or dark meat of chicken or turkey

Shellfish, smoked meats, and fish

Fried meat, fish, and eggs

Cheese, except cottage or cream cheese

DESSERTS

Bread, rice, and tapioca pudding

Vanilla ice cream, custards, and Jello

Rich pastries, pies, cakes, and desserts

Candy

BEVERAGES

Milk and cream

Malted milk and eggnog

Alcoholic and carbonated beverages

Tea and coffee, including decaffeinated coffee

MISCELLANEOUS

Macaroni, noodles, and spaghetti without sauce

Butter

Salt in moderation

Condiments

Jams and preserves containing seed, skin, or pulp

Tomato paste and catsup

Nuts, including peanut butter

Vinegar

Pancakes and waffles

HIATUS HERNIA

Hiatus hernia is a protrusion of the stomach into the chest cavity through a fistsized hole in the diaphragm, the domeshaped muscle that lies between the stomach and the chest cavity (see Figure 8). The hole has probably been there since birth, but because of muscles that weaken with age, symptoms begin in late middle age or after 65.

The symptoms of hiatus hernia mimic those of dyspepsia—gnawing abdominal pain, flatulence, and heartburn—but with one important

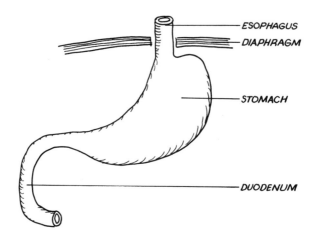

ESOPHAGUS
DIAPHRAGM
STOMACH
DUODENUM

Fig. 8. The Stomach and Duodenum

difference. In hiatus hernia, the symptoms are caused by the protrusion of the stomach through the diaphragm. When one stands, the stomach falls into place, and there is no distress, but when one lies down the stomach pops up into the chest cavity, and symptoms begin. The indigestion of hiatus hernia, therefore, is present when the patient lies down and is relieved immediately by standing up.

The treatment of hiatus hernia is directed toward neutralizing stomach acid and keeping the stomach from creeping into the chest. A bland diet is prescribed, with a generous bedtime feeding. Antispasmodics and antacids are taken at bedtime. The patient may sleep with six-inch blocks under the head of the bed to help gravity hold the stomach in the abdominal cavity. If symptoms are unrelieved by the medical measures described, the patient may be referred to a surgeon for repair, a major operation that should not be undertaken unless all medical treatment has failed.

PEPTIC ULCER

Peptic ulcer is an erosion of the lining cells of the wall of the stomach or the duodenum. The duodenum is the first part of the small intestine, lying directly beyond the stomach (see Figure 8) and receiving the direct outflow of acid as it leaves the stomach. The term peptic refers to ulcers in both the stomach and the duodenum.

The symptoms of duodenal and stomach ulcers are severe burning and gnawing pain in the upper abdomen, increased by coffee, alcoholic beverages, or spicy food and relieved by milk or antacids. Black bowel movements may be noticed if there has been internal bleeding, since the action of the stomach acid turns the iron in the blood cells black and sticky as tar.

Peptic ulcer is the final product of heredity, anxiety, anger, frustration, and dietary indiscretion. Usually the peptic ulcer sufferer has a long history of dyspepsia, which has recently become worse.

Stomach ulcers constitute one-quarter of all peptic ulcers and are significant because 10 per cent of ulcers in this location will prove to be cancerous. Therefore, peptic ulcer of the stomach must be followed carefully by repeated X-ray examinations. Duodenal ulcers make up the remaining 75 per cent of peptic ulcers. The duodenal ulcer, while just as distressing as its cousin in the stomach, never turns into cancer and need not be followed as closely with X-ray examinations.

Peptic ulcer, whether gastric or duodenal, is treated with a similar regimen. Regular doses of antispasmodic medication such as belladonna or Pro-Banthine are prescribed; antacid medication such as Maalox or Mylanta is administered at intervals of one to two hours; and the anxious patient is treated with tranquilizers such as Librium or Valium. The patient begins a strict ulcer diet program, including the following acute ulcer diet.

ACUTE PEPTIC ULCER DIET
General Diet Rules

No food to be eaten except as shown below. Feedings must be taken regularly as listed. Milk should be at room temperature. No alcoholic drinks or coffee.

8 A.M.	One portion of cooked Farina, Wheatena, or Cream of Wheat with sugar and 1/2 glass of cream. One slice of toasted white bread with butter. One glass of milk.
10 A.M.	One glass of eggnog, malted milk, buttermilk, or half and half.
12 NOON	One portion of cream soup with strained vegetables, such as celery, mushrooms, or asparagus. Mashed, baked, or boiled potato with butter. Plain Jello. Cornstarch, custard, rice, or tapioca pudding.
2 P.M.	One glass of milk.
4 P.M.	One glass of eggnog, malted milk, buttermilk, or half and half.
6 P.M.	Small cup of cream soup with vegetables. Mashed, baked, or boiled potato with butter. Small portion of

	white meat of chicken or turkey, flounder, or poached egg. One glass of milk.
8 P.M.	One glass of milk.
BEDTIME	One glass of eggnog, malted milk, buttermilk, or half and half.

If symptoms have subsided by the end of five to ten days and the bonfire in the stomach seems to have been extinguished, a change to a more liberal chronic ulcer diet is in order, as follows:

CHRONIC ULCER DIET

Drink one glass of milk between meals and at bedtime.

Foods Allowed	Foods to Be Avoided

BREADS

White bread, soda crackers, or saltines	Rye, bran, or whole wheat bread or rolls

FRUITS

Orange juice diluted with an equal amount of water	Raw fruit
All cooked fruits without tough skins	Dried fruits including dates, raisins, and figs
Ripe banana	

VEGETABLES

Pureed asparagus, carrots, spinach, peas, beets, string beans, squash	Broccoli, Brussels sprouts, cabbage, cauliflower, celery, onions, dried beans or peas
Mashed, boiled, or baked white potatoes	All raw vegetables

CEREALS

Cooked cereals, oatmeal	All dry packaged cereals
	Bran and whole wheat cereals

MEATS, POULTRY, FISH, EGGS, AND CHEESE

Roasted, broiled, or boiled lean beef, lamb, veal, ham, chicken, turkey, liver, or fish	Mutton and pork
Soft cooked eggs	Fried or spiced meats
Cottage cheese	Fried eggs
	Cheese

DESSERTS

Custards, Jello, ice cream, plain puddings, fruit whips	Cakes, pies, pastries, rich desserts

BEVERAGES

Milk, buttermilk, cocoa, Ovaltine, malted milk	Coffee, tea, carbonated beverages, alcoholic drinks, decaffeinated coffee

MISCELLANEOUS

Honey, jelly, syrups, noodles and spaghetti	Condiments, gravy, pickles, nuts, olives, popcorn, spices, vinegar, herbs, tomato paste and catsup

Most peptic ulcers will respond to therapy within a few days, but show a distressing tendency to recur. Peptic ulcers often burst into flame in the spring and fall, and those who suffer from symptoms of dyspepsia or peptic ulcer should keep a supply of medication and a copy of the diet at home, prepared to quench the ulcer fire at the first sign of symptoms.

How to prevent an ulcer:

Avoid excessive coffee, alcohol and spicy food.

Don't take on too much responsibility.

Avoid frustration and anger (easy to say, but hard to do).

Leave an hour or more each day for quiet relaxation.

Don't eat when nervous or excited.

FOOD POISONING

Food poisoning results in an acute attack of vomiting, cramps, or diarrhea that follows the ingestion of a bacterial toxin. A common source of food poisoning is staphylococcus toxin that incubates in cream doughnuts or cream pie. Salmonella food poisoning hides in creamed chicken or turkey. The source of food poisoning usually is food cooked in the morning or the day before and allowed to stand for 6 to 12 hours or more without adequate refrigeration. Epidemics sometimes follow summer picnics as homemade treats incubate in the warm sun.

The treatment of food poisoning is the relief of vomiting and diarrhea and the replacement of lost fluids. Nausea is treated with an antiemetic medication such as Compazine; the diarrhea is slowed with antispasmodic drugs such as atropine, paregoric, or Lomotil. A liquid diet is given if tolerated; if the symptoms are very severe, the patient may be admitted to the hospital for the administration of intravenous fluids.

Food poisoning is usually of brief duration, with full recovery occurring within 48 to 72 hours. If symptoms of vomiting and diarrhea persist, cultures may reveal the bacterial cause, and appropriate antibiotic therapy will be instituted.

GASTROENTERITIS

Gastroenteritis, the garden-variety intestinal virus, spares no age group, causing nausea, vomiting, diarrhea, abdominal cramps, flatulence, and fatigue. Fever may be present, and severe cases may progress to dehydration. Gastroenteritis, a highly contagious viral infection, will spread like an epidemic through a nursing home, rest home, or household.

The treatment of gastroenteritis is directed toward relief of symptoms. Vomiting is attacked by Dramamine, Compazine, or Tigan, given by injection if the patient is unable to swallow the medication. Once the patient is able to swallow, diarrhea is treated with oral medication, using Kaopectate, paregoric, or Lomotil. In severe cases the patient may require hospitalization for the intravenous administration of fluids. Gastroenteritis usually responds to therapy within three or four days, although occasional cases may persist for a week or more.

CANCER OF THE STOMACH

Cancer of the stomach is a rapidly growing, highly malignant, and particularly deadly form of cancer. Its symptoms may be nothing more than mild indigestion; when the classic picture of severe abdominal pain, weight loss, and anemia occurs, the tumor is beyond hope of cure.

All persons over 65 complaining of persistent epigastric distress should have X rays of the upper gastrointestinal tract. Although symptoms of cancer of the stomach may mimic peptic ulcer, most tumors are detectable on X-ray examination. The stomach may be observed by direct visual examination through the gastroscope, and cells may be removed from the stomach for analysis.

Ideally, cancer of the stomach is treated by surgical removal of the tumor; stomach cancer does not respond well to X-ray therapy or chemotherapy. The outlook for stomach cancer is very poor; only those cases diagnosed early in the disease will survive five years or more. The survival rate in cancer of the stomach is about 13 per cent, rather discouraging odds.

The Aging Intestines

I hav finally kum to the konklusion, that a good reliable sett ov bowels iz wurth more tu a man, than enny quantity ov brains.
HENRY WHEELER SHAW
(JOSH BILLINGS)
(1818-1885)

THE CHANGES OF AGING

The small and large intestines together are about 20 feet long. As muscles in the wall of the intestine push the food along slowly, useful nutrients are absorbed into the blood and wastes are left to be removed. The large intestine controls the amount of water that will be left in the waste products. Normal bowel movements depend upon a rhythmic muscular contraction of the wall of the large intestine; in older persons, the aged muscle does not have the vigor it once had. Sluggish bowel activity leads to constipation, diverticulosis, and other problems of age.

REGIONAL ENTERITIS

Regional enteritis, an uncommon disease, is an inflammation of the lowest part of the small intestine. Regional enteritis was publicized when it occurred in President Eisenhower during his term of office. The disease causes recurrent pain in the right lower side of the abdomen near the appendix and may be associated with weight loss, lagging appetite and, in severe cases, abscess formation. The treatment of regional enteritis is a bland diet to put the intestines to rest, antispasmodics to reduce spasm in the wall of the bowel, and antibiotics to control the formation of abscesses. Some advanced cases will require surgery.

APPENDICITIS

Appendicitis, usually considered a disease of young adults, occurs in older people with surprising frequency. The appendix is a wormlike structure attached to the first part of the large intestine, nestled in the right lower side of the abdomen. The appendix has no function in man.

Chronic constipation in older persons gives rise to small, extremely hard bits of feces called fecoliths—literally translated, a stone of feces. Fecoliths are about the size of a pea, and in older persons a fecolith can block the entrance to the appendix, causing abscess formation therein.

Appendicitis begins with pain in the right lower side of the abdomen (see Figure 9), at first intermittent in nature, but later becoming constant. There will be nausea and sometimes vomiting. Fever, although often present in the 100°–102° range, is usually not remarkable. Appendicitis causes a loss of appetite; I place great trust in the old adage that the appendicitis victim is not hungry and did not eat his last meal.

The treatment for appendicitis is immediate surgery. Once the diagnosis has been made, there is no excuse for delaying the operation even until the next morning. The presence of heart disease or emphysema should not influence the decision to operate, because without surgery the appendix will burst, and peritonitis is inevitable. With prompt detection and surgery, the recovery rate from acute appendicitis is virtually 100 per cent.

CONSTIPATION

"My bowels never move unless I take something." Constipation occurs in an aging sluggish bowel that produces small quantities of hard, dried-out feces. A low intake of fluid often contributes to constipation. The body requires a certain amount of water each day. If the quantity is sufficient, some remains in the bowels to soften the stool, but if water is in short supply, the body will claim the fluid, leaving the

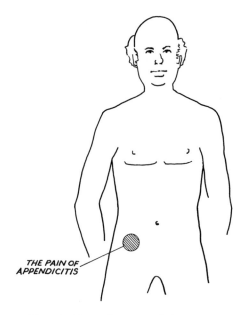

THE PAIN OF
APPENDICITIS

Fig. 9. Site of Appendicitis Pain

intestine with a desiccated hard stool. The toast, bread, soft food, and hamburger diet of older persons does not spur the bowels to move. The poor intake of water, proper fruits, and vegetables needed to stimulate the bowels is coupled with a decrease in muscle tone in the wall of the bowel to produce the torment and indignity of chronic constipation.

The bowels need not move every day. Much constipation is self-inflicted when, in a compulsive effort to have a daily bowel movement, the older person becomes dependent upon laxatives. Laxatives are useful in relief of acute constipation—four or five days without a bowel movement. If purgatives must be used, the choice should be a varied one. Milk of magnesia, the most commonly used laxative today, is bland and effective in moderate constipation. Mineral oil works to soften the stool, but its continued use can lead to deficiencies of vitamins A, D, K, and E. Phenolphthalein and cascara are stronger laxatives and should be used infrequently, while castor oil and phospho-soda are potent laxatives reserved for unusually resistant cases of constipation.

Constipation is more effectively prevented than treated. A stool softener or bulk producer, taken daily, will modify the consistency of the bowel movements. Dioctyl sulfosuccinate is a stool softener in wide use today but, in my experience, its efficacy does not justify its expense. My patients achieve better results with Metamucil or Senokot. A glass of hot water flavored with lemon is taken daily by many persons to prevent constipation and seems to work. Since dietary changes can help to relieve chronic constipation, a diet list for the treatment of chronic constipation follows.

DIET FOR CHRONIC CONSTIPATION

Foods Allowed	Foods to Be Avoided

BREADS

Whole wheat bread, biscuits, and rolls	White bread
	Soda crackers

FRUITS

Raw and stewed apples	Canned fruits
Prunes and prune juice	Fruit juices except prune juice
Raw and dried fruits, especially peaches, plums, berries, cherries, figs, dates, apricots, and grapes	

SOUPS

Any soup

VEGETABLES

Asparagus, carrots, cabbage, cauliflower, turnips, peas, eggplant, potatoes, beans, celery, tomatoes, beets, and squash	Brussels sprouts, cucumbers, onions, radishes, spinach, corn, lettuce, green beans, and lima beans

CEREALS

Dry packaged cereals, including bran flakes	Oatmeal and cooked cereals

MEATS, POULTRY, FISH, EGGS, AND CHEESE

Chicken, turkey, veal, beef or lamb	Duck, pork, and mutton
Fresh fish	Fried, canned, or spiced meats
Soft-cooked eggs	Fried eggs
	Cheese

DESSERTS

Fruit Jello and puddings, using fruits listed above	Rich cakes, pies, ice cream, pastry, and candy

BEVERAGES

Weak tea	Coffee, alcoholic beverages, milk, and cream
Skimmed milk and buttermilk	

MISCELLANEOUS

Nuts, spaghetti, macaroni, noodles,
    butter

Gravy and salad dressings
Condiments
Jellies and jams
Tomato paste and catsup

DIVERTICULOSIS AND DIVERTICULITIS

Diverticulosis of the large intestine, also called the colon, is characterized by multiple small pouches protruding from the bowel wall (see Figure 10). Diverticulosis is often the end product of many years of constipation: the bearing down and straining at stool increases the pressure within the bowel, ballooning out the weak spots in the bowel wall to form small sacs. Diverticulosis is as common as showers in April; X-ray studies of the bowels would reveal diverticulosis in about half of all people over age 65. Diverticulosis produces no symptoms in itself, but disease in the diverticuli gives rise to a condition called diverticulitis.

Diverticulitis is an inflammation or infection of these small pouches in the large intestine. A fecolith may block the opening to the diverticulum (see Figure 11), leading to an abscess, much like an appendicitis, although infection often forms without apparent cause. Severe bleeding may occur from an inflamed diverticulum.

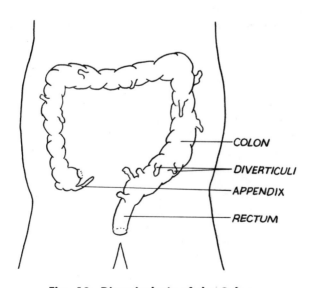

COLON
DIVERTICULI
APPENDIX
RECTUM

Fig. 10. Diverticulosis of the Colon

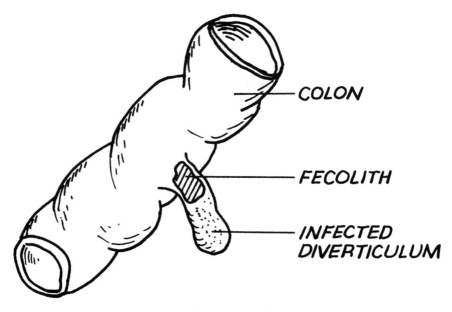

Fig. 11. Diverticulitis

The symptoms of diverticulitis are pain and bloating in the left lower side of the abdomen. There may be bleeding from the rectum; fever may occur in severe cases. Barium enema X rays of the large intestine will show the exact cause of the symptoms.

The treatment of diverticulitis includes medication to reduce spasm in the large intestine and the use of appropriate antibiotics. A liquid or bland diet is prescribed, and severe cases may require intravenous fluids. Although first or second attacks are usually treated with medication and diet, severe or recurrent episodes of diverticulitis may necessitate surgical removal of the diseased portion of the large intestine.

Help prevent diverticulosis by:
Avoiding constipation, perhaps using a stool softener.
Obeying the urge to move the bowels.
Trying not to strain at stool.

PERITONITIS

Peritonitis, an infection of the cavity containing all the abdominal organs, is usually caused by a rupture in the digestive tract. An infected appendix may burst, discharging its load of pus. A peptic ulcer may rupture, spilling stomach contents into the peritoneum surrounding the bowels. Diverticulitis of the large intestine may rupture, allowing intestinal bacteria to infect the peritoneal cavity. A gallbladder attack may build up sufficient pressure to burst the gallbladder, spilling bile into the tissues surrounding the intestines.

Peritonitis is treated with huge doses of antibiotics to control infection. The patient is given narcotics as necessary for pain, and intravenous feeding is maintained for the duration of the infection. Exceptionally severe cases have been treated by hypothermia: a freezing process to lower the temperature of the body. The cause of peritonitis, such as a perforated diverticulum, must be discovered and corrected. Peritonitis is a serious condition with a high mortality.

COLITIS

Colitis is an inflammation of the large intestine characterized by abdominal cramps, gaseousness, and alternating diarrhea or constipation. Colitis recurs as night follows day and is often related to emotional turmoil. The typical colitis victim has experienced a deprivation of some kind: loss of a loved one, sale of a home, a divorce, or even death of a cherished pet.

Treatment of colitis includes a bland diet (see pages 66-67) to rest the bowel and tranquilizers to calm the nerves. Psychotherapy is helpful in understanding the emotional basis of the disease. Antispasmodics calm spasm in the large intestine, antibiotics may be required, and cortisone is sometimes useful. A rare individual will require surgical removal of the large intestine. Colitis is a recurrent disease, related to the personality of the sufferer and his ways of handling adversity.

How to avoid colitis:
Shun spicy foods, coffee, and alcohol.
Avoid frustration and anger.
Don't push yourself too hard at work.
Avoid harsh laxatives.
Remember the value of a proper diet and adequate relaxation.

HEMORRHOIDS

Hemorrhoids are varicose veins surrounding the rectum. Common in both middle age and after 65, they often follow decades of constipation with straining at stool. Itching, burning, bleeding, and sometimes severe pain caused by enlargement signal the presence of hemorrhoids. Since they are vessels filled with blood, blood clots may form, causing sudden pain in the rectum.

Most mild hemorrhoids are treated with hot soaks, witch hazel compresses, and bland ointments or suppositories, such as Anugesic. A sitz bath (the German verb *sitzen* means to sit) involves sitting in a small tub full of hot water for 20 to 30 minutes several times a day. Severe or recurrent hemorrhoids are removed surgically, usually with welcome relief to the sufferer.

The blood clot in the hemorrhoid, which occurs suddenly and causes instant severe pain, is a special problem that can be corrected by the family doctor in the office. A small amount of Xylocaine is injected, an incision is made, and the offending blood clot pops through the incision. Following this brief office procedure, there will be discomfort for a day or two, followed by full recovery.

Here are some hints to help avoid hemorrhoids:
Avoid constipation.
Try not to strain at stool.
Avoid prolonged standing.
Don't use harsh laxatives.
Wipe gently.

RECTAL FISSURE

A rectal fissure is a crack in the skin of the rectum usually caused by passage of a large bowel movement when the rectal muscle and skin are not fully relaxed. Once a fissure is formed, each large bowel movement pulls the rent apart, and often blood is streaked on the feces.

Most rectal fissures respond to stool softeners to eliminate hard large constipated stools. Mineral oil or Metamucil may be recommended. A soothing unguent such as Medicone Rectal Ointment is applied to the rectum morning and night and following a daily sitz bath. More stubborn cases are cauterized in the office by the doctor.

RECTAL FISTULA

A fistula, a small tunnel beginning an inch or two up in the rectum and burrowing under the skin to emerge beside the rectum, begins as a small abscess that eventually drains to the outside; instead of closing, the drainage tract becomes permanent, and feces will exit through the fistula.

Rectal fistulas are treated by surgical removal under anesthesia, and the results are usually good.

CANCER OF THE LARGE INTESTINE

Cancer of the large intestine seems to be increasing in frequency. The first symptom of cancer of the large intestine is usually bleeding from the rectum, and there may be constipation, diarrhea, or crampy abdominal pain. Later symptoms of advanced cancer of the large intestine are weight loss and enlargement of the liver.

Cancer of the large intestine is treated surgically, usually with restoration of normal bowel function; in most cases, a permanent colostomy opening, requiring a bag worn on the abdominal wall, will not be needed. Some surgeons, however, use a two-stage operation with a temporary colostomy opening. Survival with cancer of the large intestine depends upon early diagnosis and prompt surgical removal. The five-year survival rate in cancer of the large intestine is about 50 per cent.

CANCER OF THE RECTUM

Cancer of the rectum causes bleeding, constipation, diarrhea, and sometimes weight loss, similar to cancer of the large intestine. Rectal cancer is diagnosed by observation with a sigmoidoscope, an instrument used by the doctor to view the last ten inches of the large intestine and rectum, allowing a specimen to be taken for analysis.

Treatment of cancer of the rectum is prompt surgical removal of the tumor. In some cases, the rectum must be closed and an opening created by a colostomy, with the bowel emptying into a bag on the abdominal wall, while in other instances normal elimination can be preserved. Survival in cancer of the rectum is dependent upon early recognition of symptoms and prompt bold surgery. The survival rate for cancer of the rectum is about 50 per cent.

The Liver
and Gallbladder
After 65

You cannot undo liver, you can take
A finger off, a leg; make and remake the
Nose, the ear, the face; break and unbreak
A compensating heart, fake and refake
A joint disabled or a stomach-ache
But liver (hepar), liver must go on
Importantly as fifth wheel in the machine
Playing its role for every body's sake.
MERRILL MOORE
(1903-1957)

THE CHANGES OF AGING

The liver, once called the body's carburetor, produces bile used in the digestion of fats and cholesterol. After formation in the liver, bile is carried to the gallbladder, which acts as a storage depot, and then is released into the intestinal tract when fats are to be digested. The aging liver continues to produce bile, but probably in smaller amounts and in a more concentrated form. The bile continues to be stored in the gallbladder; while stored, crystals of thick bile may form stones. Furthermore, the aging gallbladder becomes sluggish and empties incompletely, leaving a residue to form stones. The general slowdown in the production, storage, and release of bile from the liver sets the stage for gallstones, certain types of hepatitis, and faulty absorption of fat-soluble vitamins.

CIRRHOSIS

Cirrhosis, an inflammatory condition of the liver, is often the last chapter in a long history of heavy alcohol intake and poor nutrition. Alcohol is a liver poison and, with very few exceptions, cirrhosis is a disease of the alcoholic. The disease is common in countries where alcohol is used excessively; it was once asserted that no Frenchman could live until age 65 without acquiring cirrhosis, syphilis, or the Legion of Honor. Alcoholics will consume as much as two or three thousand calories a day as whiskey or wine, and literally do not need food for energy. The alcoholic diet is thus notoriously low in vitamins and proteins.

In the early stages of cirrhosis, normal functioning liver cells become choked by fat. As the disease progresses, the fat cells give way to nonfunctioning scar tissue, and liver failure begins.

The patient with cirrhosis shows jaundice because of faulty metabolism of bile. Spiderlike capillary formations appear under the skin, appetite is poor, fatigue is ever-present, and there may be swelling of the abdomen and feet.

Cirrhosis is treated by cessation of all use of alcohol and restoration of proper nutrition. The patient is fed a diet high in protein and low in fat, plus full doses of therapeutic vitamins. Rest in bed is advised until the jaundice has subsided.

Preventing recurrent attacks of cirrhosis of the liver calls for Spartan abstinence from the use of alcohol, plus the daily intake of a nutritious diet and therapeutic vitamins.

HEPATITIS

Hepatitis is an infection of the liver characterized by fever, pain in the liver, and jaundice. Dark urine is seen, and itching may be present as bile accumulates in the blood, urine, and tissues. There is extreme fatigue and overwhelming loss of appetite.

Hepatitis is passed from feces to fingers to food to mouth by careless toilet habits. In the 1970's hepatitis has become a disease of young people, who share food, cigarettes, and communicable diseases; older persons often contract hepatitis from younger members of the community.

Hepatitis in a person after age 65 is a serious condition, with a 5 to 10 per cent mortality. The patient should be admitted to the hospital where he can receive optimum therapy while isolated to prevent further spread of the disease. Intravenous fluid is administered if necessary to maintain hydration; therapeutic vitamins are given; and a special diet is prescribed according to the stage of the disease.

The patient with hepatitis usually feels well again within one to three months; following recovery, the use of alcohol should be forbidden for at least six months and perhaps for life.

Persons exposed to known cases of infectious hepatitis should receive protective injections of gamma globulin; however, scrupulous personal hygiene remains the most trustworthy defense against the disease.

GALLSTONES

Gallstones occur at all ages, but are particularly common in elderly sluggish gallbladders. A stone in the gallbladder may act as a ball valve, blocking the exit of bile when the gallbladder tries to empty in response to the presence of fat in the intestine (see Figure 12). Thus, when the gallstone sufferer eats fats, the gallbladder contracts against an opening blocked by a stone, and pain in the right upper side of the abdomen occurs. Sometimes a very tiny stone will be released from the gallbladder to block the bile duct between the gallbladder and the small intestine, causing jaundice and fever.

The treatment of gallstones is surgical removal of the gallbladder, although antispasmodic medication such as atropine may give temporary relief during an attack. A low-fat diet is prescribed, averting further attacks until a surgical date is arranged. The removal of the

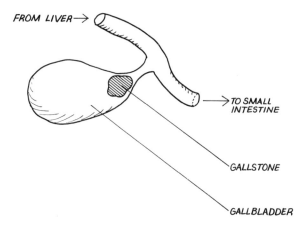

FROM LIVER→

→TO SMALL INTESTINE

GALLSTONE

GALLBLADDER

Fig. 12. Obstructing Gallstone

gallbladder is a one- to two-hour major operation necessitating about ten days in the hospital; following surgery, the patient should feel total relief of symptoms and be allowed to indulge in previously forbidden culinary treats.

Can gallstones be prevented? Perhaps not always, because of the hereditary pattern, but it may help to keep slim, take plenty of fluids, and eat a minimum of fats and cholesterol.

CANCER OF THE LIVER

Cancer of the liver may represent the spread of cancer from another organ such as the stomach, bowel, or lung. On the other hand, cancer of the liver may also be a hepatoma, a cancer arising in the organ itself. The symptoms of both these conditions are similar and will be described together.

Cancer of the liver causes pain, jaundice, and enlargement of the organ. Weight loss will be noted, along with a marked loss of appetite. Periodic physical examination will reveal a progressively enlarging liver, with pain upon palpation.

The outlook for carcinoma of the liver is very poor, except in those isolated cases where a small hepatoma tumor can be removed surgically. Liver cancer does not respond to X-ray therapy, although a few fortunate individuals will show temporary remission with the use of chemotherapeutic drugs such as nitrogen mustard injected intravenously.

More than half of all hepatomas will be found in livers previously affected by cirrhosis. Since cirrhosis, in turn, is attributable to heavy drinking, the first step in preventing primary liver cancer is the temperate use of alcoholic beverages.

The Senior Citizen and His Heart

*The heart is the only organ that takes no
rest. That is why it is so good.*
MARTIN H. FISCHER
(1879-1962)

PRESBYCARDIA

Presbycardia is the disease process that accompanies the aging heart.
The heart is a muscular pump, propelling blood throughout the body
(see Figure 13). Blood is brought to the heart by the veins. The heart
then pumps the blood through the lungs, where it picks up oxygen and
gives up carbon dioxide before returning to the heart. Next the heart
pumps the blood through the aorta to the remainder of the body,
carrying the all-important oxygen to the vital organs. Valves within the
heart prevent the backflow of the blood between beats.

With advancing age, the heart becomes somewhat flabby, and each
heartbeat pumps out a little less blood. Arteriosclerosis strikes the tiny
blood vessels supplying the heart with oxygen, and the heart muscle can
suffer an oxygen shortage during exercise. The heart valves, which
prevent backflow of blood, acquire deposits of cholesterol and calcium
and no longer close tightly. The diminished output of blood per beat
and the backflow of blood through leaking valves impair the efficiency
of the heart; the aging organ cannot pump all the blood that is carried

87

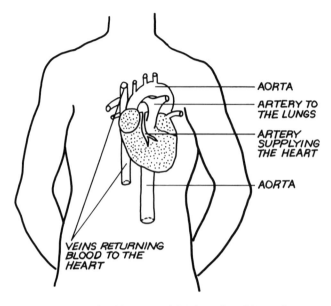

Fig. 13. The Heart and Major Blood Vessels

back to it by the veins; and fluid begins to back up in the veins of the pelvis, legs, and lungs.

EDEMA

Edema means fluid in the tissues, often caused by failure of the heart to pump blood efficiently. Backup of blood in the veins of the legs, pelvis, and lungs causes the fluid of the bloodstream to move into the tissues, where it is seen as swollen ankles, pelvic congestion, and shortness of breath when climbing the stairs. Edema in the lungs is most noticeable at night as fluid seeks the lowest level. During the day, the fluid pools in the ankles and the pelvis, but when one lies down at night, the fluid responds to gravity, filling the lungs and causing shortness of breath. The patient with early heart failure awakens from sleep because of difficulty in breathing and finds relief by arising and sitting in a chair.

HEART MURMURS

Heart murmurs are sounds made by the turbulence of the blood passing through the valves of the heart, similar to the babbling of a brook as it rushes through a narrow channel. While many murmurs occur because of childhood heart disease, murmurs may begin after 65, usually caused by minor heart attacks, with damage to the supporting structure of the valves.

Leakage occurs when the valves do not close tightly between heartbeats. Damaged, thickened, or structurally weakened heart valves will close incompletely, allowing blood to leak back between heartbeats and compromising the heart's efficiency.

Although heart murmurs are sounds that require no specific treatment, they usually indicate a leaking heart valve; there may be mild heart failure necessitating salt restriction, diuretics to eliminate excess fluid from the blood, and digitalis to strengthen the force of the heartbeat. Severe valvular leakage may require open heart surgery; yet many heart murmurs are present for decades without provoking the first hint of trouble.

CONGESTIVE HEART FAILURE

Congestive heart failure is a backup of blood in the lungs and veins of the body. The term heart failure refers to the inability of the heart to pump the blood through the circulatory system as fast as it is received from the veins. The symptoms of congestive heart failure are shortness of breath upon minor exertion, the need for three or four pillows to sleep, and awaking in the middle of the night with shortness of breath as fluid accumulates in the lungs. Swollen ankles occur often, and there may be puffiness about the hands and legs.

Congestive heart failure is a very common disease of persons over 65. A mild form of congestive heart failure must be considered a logical extension of the normal aging process of the heart; most of my octogenarian and nonagenarian nursing home patients require treatment for mild chronic congestive heart failure.

The disability is treated with digitalis to increase the efficiency of the heart and with diuretics to drain excess fluid from the tissues and blood. Increased rest is prescribed during the acute phase, a daily nap is often helpful, and weight reduction of the obese is mandatory.

Because salt increases the fluid content of the blood, a salt-restriction diet is prescribed. The following is a low salt diet that has been useful in my practice.

LOW SALT DIET

Foods Allowed	Foods to Be Avoided
BREADS	
White bread	Crackers, pancakes, and waffles
FRUITS	
Any fresh or stewed unsweetened fruit	Bananas, dates, raisins
Fresh fruit juice	Canned fruit or juice
SOUPS	
Any fresh soup, except beef, celery, or spinach	All canned soups
	All meat-stock soups, bouillons, and broths
	Celery or spinach soup
VEGETABLES	
All fresh vegetables, except spinach, beets, and beet greens	All canned vegetables
	Spinach, beets, beet greens, sauerkraut, and vegetable juices
CEREALS	
Cooked cereals	All other cereals
Oatmeal, barley, corn, and rice cereals	
MEATS, POULTRY, FISH, EGGS, AND CHEESE	
Baked, broiled, or boiled lamb, beef, veal, chicken, turkey, or fresh fish	All canned, processed, cured, or smoked meats
Soft cooked eggs	Corned beef, sausage, ham, bacon, and cheese
Cottage cheese	Shellfish and salted fish
	Cheese
DESSERTS	
Any fresh or stewed fruit	All rich desserts, including cake, pie, and pastry
Gelatin	
BEVERAGES	
Coffee and tea	Mineral water, alcohol, carbonated beverages
Small quantities of whole or skimmed milk	Water treated in water-softening equipment.
Bottled spring water	
MISCELLANEOUS	
Sugar or honey (sparingly)	Pickles, olives, baking soda, salad dressing, jelly, catsup, prepared mustard, and horseradish
Unsalted butter	
Unsalted nuts	Salted nuts
Noodles and spaghetti	

How about the prevention of congestive heart failure? You can't correct a leaking heart valve without surgery, *but it helps to:*

Shed excess weight.

Consume as little salt as possible.

Rest a half hour morning and afternoon, with legs elevated.

Avoid exposure to colds and flu.

Avoid extreme exertion, such as shoveling snow or pushing a stalled car.

Treat viruses and colds promptly.

Exercise each day within limits prescribed by your doctor.

PERICARDITIS

Pericarditis is an inflammation of the outer lining of the heart. It is not a common condition, but its recognition is important because it can mimic more serious heart conditions such as heart attack. Pericarditis causes a sharp pain in the front of the chest, characteristically less intense when the patient leans forward from the waist. There may be a low-grade fever and shortness of breath. The doctor will diagnose pericarditis following careful examination, an electrocardiogram, and blood tests. Pericarditis is treated with rest and antiinflammatory drugs or antibiotics as necessary. Most cases of pericarditis recover completely within several weeks.

IRREGULAR RHYTHMS OF THE HEART

The normal heart beats rhythmically 50 to 90 times a minute. As described by Leonardo da Vinci in the 15th century, "The heart . . . moves of itself and does not stop unless forever." The normal heartbeat arises in response to an electric impulse that passes over the heart and can be recorded on the electrocardiogram. The aging heart often has small areas of scar tissue that can detour the electric impulses, causing irregular heart rhythms, including fibrillation, where the heartbeat is totally irregular (see Figure 14); flutter, where one half of the heart beats more rapidly than the other; and other obscure rhythms that are diagnosed with the electrocardiogram.

Many persons with irregular heartbeat of long standing are not treated; the doctor reasons, "Let's not upset the applecart." Fibrillation known to be of recent origin may be treated with electric stimulation of the heart: the application of high-voltage electric shock to the chest for a brief period while the patient is under sedation. Drug therapy

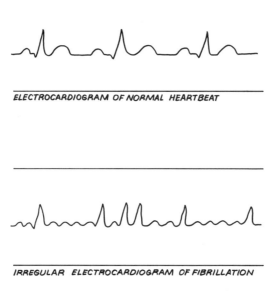

ELECTROCARDIOGRAM OF NORMAL HEARTBEAT

IRREGULAR ELECTROCARDIOGRAM OF FIBRILLATION

Fig. 14. Electrocardiographic Recordings

for irregular rhythms includes medications such as digitalis, quinidine, procainamide, Inderal, and potassium. Irregular rhythms of the heart vary from nuisance to life-threatening, depending upon their extent.

ANGINA PECTORIS

Angina pectoris is a viselike pain in the chest caused by a temporary shortage of blood to the heart. The heart is nourished by two major blood vessels that service the front and back of the organ; with a hardening of these arteries, there is a decrease in the blood available to the heart muscle. While the affected heart performs well under ordinary circumstances, such increased demands as exertion, large meals, emotional turmoil, or cold weather can exert a strain on the heart that cannot be met by the blood supply available to it.

All muscles that lack nutrient-bearing blood complain by causing pain; angina pectoris is a straining heart's cry for air. Angina pectoris itself does not cause permanent damage to the heart, but its presence warns that the heart suffers from a marginal blood supply.

Angina pectoris is treated with rest and medication to increase blood flow to the heart muscle. Nitroglycerin, taken under the tongue, will act within two minutes to improve blood flow to the heart. The reaction to nitroglycerin is brief—probably about 20 to 30 minutes—

and after that time the medication may be repeated. Chronic angina sufferers with many attacks each day have been treated with such long-acting medications to increase blood flow to the heart as Peritrate, Isordil, or Cardilate. In stubborn cases, Inderal has been used with good results. Overweight patients must reduce, and regular rest periods during the day are often helpful. Occasionally, surgical repair of the deficient blood supply to the heart is performed.

The angina patient must avoid the combination of cold weather, exertion, large meals, and aggravation. That means that snow-covered sidewalks are to be shoveled by teenagers, stalled cars pulled by tow trucks, second helpings at mealtime refused, and harsh words met with the smile of equanimity.

HEART ATTACK

Of all the ailments which may blow out life's
little candle, heart disease is the chief
WILLIAM BOYD
Pathology for the Surgeon

A heart attack differs from angina pectoris chiefly in that permanent damage occurs in the former. The pain of the heart attack is an oppressive feeling in the middle of the chest, often radiating to the chin or down the arm (see Figure 15), often associated with shortness of breath and nausea. The pain may begin while exerting, after a large meal, or with no apparent cause. The victim will usually realize that this is a different and more severe pain than his usual angina; the failure of relief after several nitroglycerin tablets should prompt a call to the doctor.

The heart attack, which the doctor may call a myocardial infarction or coronary occlusion, will be diagnosed by physical examination, electrocardiogram, and blood tests. In about half of all cases, the initial examination is inconclusive, and the final diagnosis will await repeated electrocardiograms and blood tests. During this time, however, the patient will probably be admitted to the hospital and placed in a special coronary care unit.

The coronary care unit has dramatically improved the odds against heart attack. Heart attack victims who survive the first few minutes and reach the hospital alive stand a much better chance of surviving today than they did ten years ago. The coronary care unit has the most

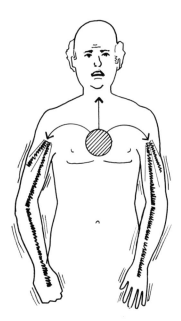

Fig. 15. Site and Radiation of Heart Attack Pain

modern devices for measuring blood pressure, respiration, pulse rate, and other vital signs. Electrodes are placed on the chest to record each heartbeat on an electronic monitor; a heart rate above or below a certain figure will trigger an alarm and bring instant aid. Although not needed in the treatment of most heart attacks, modern therapeutic drugs and instruments are readily available for any emergency. The coronary care nurse is a highly trained individual who has often spent time in a medical teaching center studying electrocardiograms and emergency resuscitative techniques.

Bed rest plus the prevention of further blood clotting is the cornerstone of therapy. The heart attack victim may expect to spend three weeks or more in the hospital, the first week in the coronary care unit, followed by a transfer to a general hospital bed. During the acute phase of the heart attack, intravenous fluid is often administered continuously, and the doctor may decide to "thin out the blood" to prevent the formation of further blood clots in the heart or phlebitis in the legs. Because of the boredom of enforced bed rest, a mild tranquilizer will usually be prescribed. Demerol or morphine will be ordered if necessary for pain, oxygen will be administered as needed, and irregularities of the heart rhythm may require lidocaine, digitalis, or quinidine. Most heart attack victims will miss three or four months of work. The heart attack victim must give up smoking totally and forever.

If blood tests have shown a high level of cholesterol or fats, the physician may prescribe a low cholesterol diet, such as the following diet list, which has been useful in my practice.

LOW CHOLESTEROL DIET

Foods Allowed	Foods to Be Avoided
BREADS	
Breads not made with egg yolk, cream, or solid shortening	Bread made with egg yolk, cream, or solid shortening
FRUITS	
Any fresh, cooked, canned, or frozen fruit or fruit juice	
SOUPS	
All soups without meat or cream stock	Meat and cream stock soups
VEGETABLES	
All vegetables	Vegetables cooked with butter
CEREALS	
All cereals	Cereals with cream
MEATS, POULTRY, FISH, EGGS, AND CHEESE	
Baked, boiled, or broiled veal, lean beef, lamb, chicken, turkey, and fish	Pork, duck, oysters, shrimp, liver, and sweetbreads
Cottage cheese	Eggs, cheese, butter, animal fats, lard, and solid shortening
DESSERTS	
Gelatin and sherbet	Ice cream and whipped cream
Pastry, pudding made without egg yolk, cream, or solid shortening	Pastry, pudding, and cake made with egg yolk, cream, or solid shortening
BEVERAGES	
Skimmed milk	Whole milk, cream, and eggnog
Tea and coffee without cream	
Alcoholic beverages and soft drinks in moderation	
MISCELLANEOUS	
French or vinegar dressing	Mayonnaise, gravy, and nuts
Sugar, syrup, or honey	Solid shortening, hydrogenated margarine. butter, and lard
Noodles, macaroni, and spaghetti	
Mustard and catsup	
Liquid shortening and nonhydrogenated margarine	

The typical heart attack victim has a long family history of hardening of the arteries, is overweight, exercises too little, and works at a high level of nervous tension. He usually eats too many dairy products and fatty meats, both high in cholesterol.

Can angina and heart attacks be prevented? Yes, in many cases, *if the following rules are heeded:*

Stay slim.

Exercise regularly, within limits prescribed by the doctor.

Minimize the intake of dairy products and fatty meats.

Don't put in too many hours at work.

Take vacations regularly.

Allow a little time for relaxation each day.

Don't smoke.

Circulation
in the
Senior Citizen

THE AGING BLOOD VESSELS

The blood vessels carry oxygen, glucose, protein, and other nutrients to all cells of the body. Probably no other organ system is as important in the changes of aging as the blood vessels. All aging vessels show some degree of hardening: the accumulation of fat, cholesterol, and calcium in the walls of the arteries that diminishes the elasticity of the vessel. Arteriosclerosis reduces the diameter of the blood vessel so that less blood can flow to vital organs. Americans with diets high in fats and cholesterol show much more arteriosclerosis than do Orientals, who eat little fat-containing food; overwork, anxiety, and inactivity aggravate progressive hardening of Western man's arteries.

VARICOSE VEINS

Varicosities are swollen veins full of blood, most commonly occurring in the legs. The blood is carried down the legs by arteries under pressure from the heart, but must wend its way back up through the veins. The veins have a series of valves to maintain one-way flow and prevent the blood from rushing downhill into the feet under the pull of gravity. Here's where the trouble begins. Varicose vein sufferers have damaged valves. Normally, muscular motion of the legs pumps the blood uphill through healthy veins from one valve set to another, but with varicose veins, the impaired valves allow the blood to leak through and collect in the feet and ankles.

Varicose veins are treated with periodic rest, with the feet elevated to drain the veins. Support stockings should be worn at all times when standing, and severe cases will require Ace elastic bandages. Failure of these measures to control the varicose veins adequately should prompt their surgical removal.

Prevent varicose veins from developing by:
Staying slim.
Avoiding tight circular garters.
Resting with the legs elevated each afternoon.
Exercising daily.

HARDENING OF THE ARTERIES

Hardening of the arteries, caused by accumulations of fat, cholesterol, and calcium in their walls, can result in severe damage to the feet and legs in some cases. Advanced hardening of the arteries to the legs can reduce blood flow below the critical point needed to repair damaged cells, and affected persons often complain of claudication: pain in the legs after walking a specific distance such as 40 or 50 yards and relieved by rest. Many elderly people on the street who appear to be window shopping are really stopping to relieve their claudication pain. Infection of the feet is extremely dangerous to the person with hardened arteries, because the feet lack sufficient healing blood to combat infection, and a small abscess can progress to gangrene.

Hardening of the arteries to the legs is often treated with medications such as papaverine or Arlidin to open up blood vessels. Overweight persons must reduce, and a program of regular exercise to increase blood flow to the legs is often prescribed. The use of tobacco in all forms is forbidden; this is a most important step in therapy. In isolated cases, blockage of small segments of the artery can be removed surgically.

Hardening of the arteries may be a family trait; however, because the condition causes so many of the problems of aging, *these attempts at prevention are worth the effort:*

Keep the weight down.
Avoid cholesterol and fats in the diet.
Exercise regularly.
Don't smoke.

HYPERTENSION

Hypertension means elevated blood pressure; because it is related to hardening of the arteries, high blood pressure is exceedingly common after age 65. Blood pressure, measured in millimeters of mercury, is recorded as systolic pressure (the thrust of force from the heart) and diastolic (the pressure in the arteries between beats). Normal blood pressure is below 150 mm of mercury systolic and below 100 mm diastolic.

Elevated blood pressure may cause no complaints until its presence is revealed by nosebleed or a stroke; in some individuals, however, it may cause symptoms such as dizziness and headache. The characteristic headache of high blood pressure is an early morning "full" headache in the back of the head. Blood pressure often affects several branches of the family tree, and there is a definite tendency for elevated blood pressure, hardening of the arteries, diabetes mellitus, and heart attacks to occur in members of the same family.

High blood pressure is treated with many different kinds of medication. Because it is related to excess salt and fluid in the bloodstream, the initial attack upon blood pressure will include salt restriction in the diet, perhaps supplemented by the prescription of a diuretic pill such as Diuril, Hygroton, or Aldactone. If these measures are not sufficient to control the blood pressure, more potent medications such as reserpine may be added. Reserpine was discovered many centuries ago in India and used as a tranquilizer long before its value in elevated blood pressure was discovered.

Reserpine has the disadvantage of causing depression in some patients, a possible side effect that the doctor must weigh against the drug's advantages. Aldomet is a stronger blood pressure medication taken two to four times daily. Ismelin, usually reserved for stubborn cases not responsive to milder medication, can cause patients to feel lightheaded if they stand quickly. The treatment of hypertension also includes reduction of obesity; dairy products should be avoided to reduce the body's cholesterol level.

The hypertensive patient should visit his physician at regular intervals to maintain control of the blood pressure and prevent the undetected elevation that may cause a stroke.

How to help prevent high blood pressure:

Maintain your ideal weight.

Keep the salt intake down.

Watch the fats and cholesterol that lead to hardening of the arteries.

Don't smoke.

Exercise regularly.

Maintain the proper balance of work and relaxation.

Develop equanimity and a sense of humor so that minor irritations do not become major crises.

STROKE

A stroke strikes like summer lightning out of a clear sky. There is bleeding or a blood clot in one of the small arteries of the brain, and the portion of the brain served by this artery ceases to function. Because different parts of the brain control the muscles and nerves of certain areas of the body, a stroke will cause immediate loss of function in the corresponding parts of the body. The victim of a major stroke

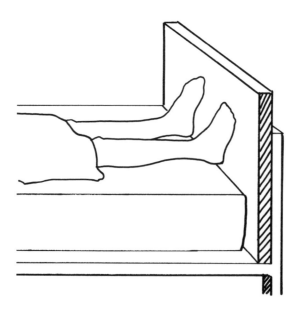

Fig. 16. Footboard to Prevent Stiff Ankle Tendons

may have a sudden convulsion or loss of consciousness, plus a weakness of one side of the face, one arm, and one leg.

The patient with a severe stroke should be admitted to the hospital, preferably in a unit specifically designed for treatment and rehabilitation of such disabilities. Persons unable to eat will be fed intravenously, with vitamins given to supplement nutrition. The paralyzed limbs will be carefully positioned and will be passively exercised several times daily to prevent stiffened joints. Vasodilators, medication to improve blood flow to the brain, may be prescribed by the doctor to bolster circulation to the remaining brain cells. The patient will be turned frequently in bed and his position changed to prevent bedsores. A footboard to keep the blankets from holding the feet extended will help to prevent stiffening of the ankle tendons (see Figure 16), and a rolled washcloth in the paralyzed hand helps preserve normal function (see Figure 17). Recovery from the acute phase of the stroke usually takes three to seven days, after which time many patients will be more alert, eat soft food, and begin rehabilitation.

Rehabilitation includes physical and speech therapy and vocational rehabilitation. As a rule, the right-handed person who has a stroke involving the right arm and leg will also have impaired speech, but the right-handed person with a stroke on the left side of the body

Fig. 17. A Rolled Washcloth Prevents Hand Contracture

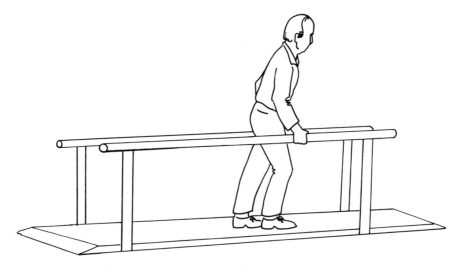

Fig. 18. Learning to Walk with Parallel Bars

will usually not show a speech disorder. If the speech is impaired, the patient should have the services of a speech therapist on a regular basis. Daily physical therapy should be started in the hospital, with electric stimulation of paralyzed muscles, active and passive exercise of the involved side, and progressive ambulation leading to walking, first with parallel bars (see Figure 18), then with a walker, and eventually with a cane. The ability to walk again without a cane or walker should be the goal. Vocational therapy is prescribed to keep the hands and mind busy; leather work or knitting can help to pass idle hours while recovering from the stroke.

The recovery from a stroke is often slow. Following a person's hospitalization for the acute attack and after he begins physical therapy, the family and physician may decide to place the patient in a nursing home for continued physical therapy and exercise. Usually after weeks or months of therapy, the patient can walk out the door and home.

Because strokes are related to hardening of the arteries and hypertension, the prevention of stroke requires careful regulation of blood pressure, weight control, and reduction of dietary fats and cholesterol.

The Aging Lung

Some folk seem glad even to draw their breath.
WILLIAM MORRIS
(1834-1896)

Diseases of the lungs abound in senior citizens. Let us consider the structure of the respiratory system and how it works (see Figure 19). The lungs comprise millions of tiny air sacs, having an appearance and consistency very much like those of a rubber sponge. The lungs transfer oxygen to the blood and remove carbon dioxide waste products. Air passes into the lungs through bronchi—tubes connecting the lungs with the nose, throat, and the outside world. Once inside the lungs, oxygen in the air passes through the thin lining of the sacs into blood capillaries. The same capillary blood gives up its carbon dioxide waste, which is then exhaled from the lungs and expelled from the body.

The lungs work as a bellows. Inhaling uses the muscles of the chest wall to enlarge the rib cage, creating a lower air pressure within the lungs, and air from the outside rushes in to fill the vacuum. Exhaling relaxes the muscles of the chest wall, allowing the chest to fall back to a resting position that forces air out of the lungs. To perform these functions efficiently, the lungs must have elasticity.

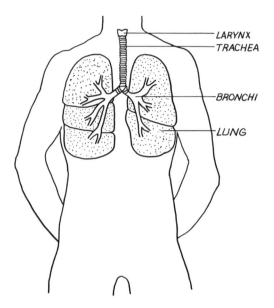

LARYNX
TRACHEA
BRONCHI
LUNG

Fig. 19. The Respiratory System

THE CHANGES OF AGING

With age, the lungs lose their elasticity and become more rigid, so that inhalation is not quite so deep and exhalation less than complete. The aging lungs assume a position of partial inflation, preventing full inhalation of nourishing oxygen and full exhalation of carbon dioxide waste products.

Recurrent coughing breaks down the walls between the air sacs; each cough shatters a few tiny walls, so that many small efficient air sacs become one large flabby inefficient cavity. The air sacs thus become fewer in number, but larger in volume. There is a subsequent decrease in the amount of capillary blood passing through the air sacs, and less oxygen is picked up by the blood. The cells, starving for oxygen, voice their complaint as fatigue. Larger air sacs do not contract well during exhalation, with a further buildup of carbon dioxide waste products in the blood.

The loss of elasticity and the breakdown of small air sacs is a gradual process and is compatible with a long (if short-winded) life, unless aggravated by one of the diseases we will discuss next. Severe and recurrent coughing greatly speeds the breakdown of air sacs and brings about such diseases as bronchitis or emphysema.

BRONCHITIS

Bronchitis, an inflammation of the cells lining the bronchial air tubes, is caused by infection or chronic irritation following inhalation of some noxious substance. In this age of antibiotics, chronic bronchitis caused by infection is indeed rare and is almost always related to inhalation of toxic particles, notably tobacco smoke. There can be no question that the growing and excessive use of tobacco in cigarettes, cigars, and pipes over the last several decades has led to an epidemic of chronic bronchitis in our elderly citizens. Although this bronchitis is worsened by other noxious elements such as exhaust fumes and industrial pollution, tobacco smoke remains the chief offender. The incidence of chronic bronchitis would be radically decreased if all cigarette smoking were to cease.

Those who suffer from chronic bronchitis have a hacking cough that worsens early in the morning and shortness of breath upon exertion. There may be recurrent fever and fatigue. Untreated chronic bronchitis will progress gradually into pulmonary emphysema.

The successful treatment of chronic bronchitis demands total cessation of tobacco smoking and removal of the patient from other sources of air pollution. Expectorant cough medicines such as glycerol guaiacolate or elixir terpin hydrate are often helpful, but codeine-containing expectorants should be used with caution because they suppress the cough reflex that is important in clearing excessive mucus out of the lungs.

The patient should take six full glasses of water each day to keep the mucus loose. Postural drainage, which consists of nothing more than lying face down over the side of the bed with the chest leaning down to the floor, helps clear mucus from the chest early in the morning. Intermittent episodes of fever and severe cough that represent acute bacterial infection should be treated by the doctor with appropriate antibiotics.

Steps to help prevent bronchitis:
Don't smoke.
Avoid dusty areas.
Treat all colds promptly.
Take plenty of fluids to keep phlegm moist.
Remember the value of adequate nutrition and proper rest.

EMPHYSEMA

Pulmonary emphysema is usually the end result of many years of repeated coughing, commonly attributable to chronic bronchitis which, in turn, is most often caused by heavy smoking. The emphysema victim is recognized by his barrel chest, which is unusually thick from front to back, representing a loss of the normal elasticity of the lungs. The patient suffers from recurrent episodes of shortness of breath upon slight exertion and, in the worst stages, gasps for air, even when resting. There is a recurrent hacking cough, worse early in the morning after the patient has been reclining at night, productive of thick sticky sputum. The patient is often short of breath when lying flat in bed and will frequently find relief by sleeping in a chair at night.

The treatment of pulmonary emphysema centers around relief of the chronic bronchial irritation and the provision of oxygen to the remaining air sacs. All use of tobacco, which William Cowper aptly called a "pernicious weed," must cease. Expectorant cough medicines, as outlined in the section on chronic bronchitis, are helpful, and postural drainage is most beneficial in emphysema patients. Regular deep breathing exercises help open collapsed air sacs; air conditioning, particularly in the bedroom, is a great help.

A large number of devices has been developed to aid the emphysema patient's breathing. Hand nebulizers and self-contained units can be purchased either over the counter or by doctor's prescription. The most ambitious unit is the intermittent positive pressure breathing apparatus (IPPB), which is found in hospitals and has recently been adapted for home use. The IPPB unit forces air and prescribed medication into the lungs under pressure, opening up tiny collapsed air sacs that previously had languished. The machine also helps wash out thick sputum trapped in the lungs. Patients with pulmonary emphysema are very susceptible to infections of the lungs and suffer recurrent episodes of colds, bronchitis, and pneumonia.

How to prevent emphysema:
Don't smoke tobacco in any form.
Avoid dust, fumes, and other respiratory irritants.
Treat all colds, coughs, and allergies promptly.
Exercise regularly, including deep breathing exercises.

PNEUMONIA

Pneumonia is a bacterial infection of a segment of the lung, occurring most commonly in individuals with other illness, such as bronchitis, emphysema, severe flu, or extreme debility. Pneumonia is often fatal to moribund elderly patients.

Pneumonia causes severe cough, high fever, shortness of breath, and often a dusky complexion of the skin caused by a shortage of oxygen in the blood. These symptoms in any person, young or old, shout "Danger!" and the doctor should be notified at once.

Pneumonia is treated with penicillin or one of its substitutes, expectorants to liquefy phlegm, and aspirin for fever. Patients with pneumonia are usually treated in the hospital, where they can receive X-ray examinations, cultures to determine the exact type of infection, antibiotics by injection if needed, and oxygen. Only an occasional mild case is amenable to home care by a dedicated family and conscientious physician. Pneumonia in the elderly carries a significant mortality, and any suspected lung infection should be called to the attention of the doctor immediately.

ASTHMA

Asthma is a form of bronchial congestion with wheezing, a whistling sound heard when exhaling. Asthma occurs in episodes; the patient feels fit most of the time, but suffers short periods of disabling chest congestion. Allergy, heredity, colds, weather changes, and emotional upsets all induce an asthma attack. Indeed, the person who is hereditarily prone to asthma may feel in good health for many months until he encounters the unhappy combination of a smoke-filled room or a common cold on a muggy humid day when he has a disagreement with his wife.

The asthma patient will be seen sitting quietly leaning on his elbows, a position in which he can most efficiently use his chest muscles to breathe. He does not walk around because every bit of energy must be used to pump air in and out of the lungs. The patient appears anxious, and a dry cough is present.

Treatment of the acute asthma attack includes water to liquefy phlegm, expectorant cough medicines to help loosen secretions, and drugs such as theophylline, aminophylline, and ephedrine to open the bronchial tubes. Adrenalin is often given by injection or inhaler, but the doctor will weigh Adrenalin's advantages against the possibility of such side effects as rapid heartbeat and irregularity of the heart. Hand nebulizers containing Adrenalin or similar potent drugs should be used with caution. Elderly asthmatics should not be allowed to keep an inhaler at their bedside, sucking on it like a pacifier, and with each dose pumping Adrenalin into the blood, straining the heart and raising the blood pressure. The judicious use of cortisone is frequently helpful in treating an acute attack of asthma, but its long-term use should be discouraged.

The prevention of asthma includes the careful choice of allergy-free ancestors, the avoidance of colds and emotional disturbances, the use of air conditioning and air purifiers, and, on occasion, allergy injections. Smoky dust-filled rooms and areas with a high pollen count are danger zones. Very allergic asthmatics should banish all animals from the house and replace dust-collecting drapes and carpets with shades and vinyl tile. The asthmatic patient must not, and in most cases cannot, smoke.

TUBERCULOSIS

Pulmonary tuberculosis, which Henry David Thoreau called "the hectic glow of consumption," is becoming a disease of the past in young and middle-aged people. However, occasional elderly persons have carried hidden tuberculosis pockets in their lungs for many years, thinking their symptoms to be a cigarette cough or chronic bronchitis. The true condition is often discovered only if the patient has occasion to be hospitalized and when skin tests and appropriate bacteriological studies are done. The incidence of these undetected cases of tuberculosis in elderly persons becomes significant when a child is found to have tuberculosis and members of the household are X-rayed. In almost every such case a senior family member is found to have active pulmonary tuberculosis.

When found, the active tuberculosis victim is often admitted to a tuberculosis sanatorium to receive chemical therapy for weeks or months. Known close household contacts may be followed with X rays, although the doctor may recommend prophylactic therapy with isoniazid hydrochloride tablets, perhaps for as long as one year. With improved chemotherapy, the extensive surgical procedures once performed on tuberculosis patients are becoming outdated, as the disease itself should become extinct with improved methods of detection and treatment.

CARCINOMA OF THE LUNG

Cancer of the lung is a malignant, fast-growing tumor. When the patient first develops symptoms of cough, anemia, weight loss, and fatigue, the cancer is already too far advanced to be curable. The small percentage of cures—about 8 per cent—achieved by various means occur in those tumors diagnosed early as unexpected findings on routine chest X-ray examinations.

Cancer of the lung has been treated with surgery, radiation therapy, and chemotherapy—the injection of chemicals into the bloodstream. Traditionally, the cases that are considered to be curable—small tumors without symptoms such as weight loss or anemia—are surgically removed. Tumors too far advanced to be removed are often given radiation therapy, while chemotherapy is often a last desperate resort. The outlook for the patient with carcinoma of the lung is bleak, indeed, with an average life expectancy of nine to twelve months once the diagnosis is made. Because lung cancer is virtually unknown in nonsmokers, the prevention of this devastating disease really depends on the abolition of cigarette smoking.

The Aging Skin

*If you've got a mole above your chin, you'll
never be beholden to your kin.*
Old English Rhyme

THE SKIN GROWS OLDER

The epidermis is composed of three layers: the deepest germ cell layer
where new cells are produced; the actively growing layer that is closer
to the surface; and the outermost thickened layer where old discarded
cells form a protective barrier (see Figure 20). Pigment cells are located
in the deepest layer. Beneath the epidermis is the dermis containing the
hair follicles, nerve endings, blood vessels, fat cells, sweat glands, and
oil-producing sebaceous glands.

The character of the skin changes at different times during life.
The growing teenager has a very oily skin peppered with plugged
sebaceous glands and acne pimples. After the teenage skin crisis, the
complexion clears until after middle age, when the normal protective
secretions of the skin glands begin to dwindle. In colder climates, the
aging skin may show a dry flaking condition colloquially called the
winter itch, characterized by a relative thickness of the outer scaling
layer of cells. The loss of protective secretions, the scant secretion of
sebaceous material, and the increased thickness of the outer scaling

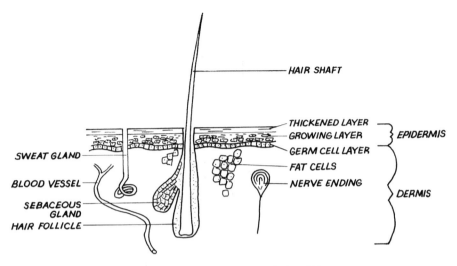

Fig. 20. The Anatomy of the Skin

layer of skin may predispose to some diseases that we will discuss in this chapter.

SEBORRHEA

Seborrhea, a name derived from the two Greek words for "flow" and "fat," is an oily flaking condition found on the scalp, face, and the middle of the chest. The most common form of seborrhea is dandruff, a dry itching of the scalp and eyebrows. In dandruff, excessive oiliness combines with an abnormally thickened outer layer of skin to produce a veneer of flaking scales.

The treatment for dandruff is regular shampooing with special products that dissolve the greasy scales. One very widely used shampoo for this purpose is selenium sulfide, sold under the brand name of Selsun, for which a prescription is required, or Selsun Blue, milder and available without prescription. For less troublesome dandruff, Sebulex is often effective. Since a tar compound will dissolve the oily scales of dandruff, Zetar Shampoo is often very effective. Seborrhea scales about the body are often treated with a combination of crude coal tar and hydrocortisone, such as Zetone Cream.

HAIR LOSS

Hair loss appears in two forms: normal male patterns of baldness and hair loss caused by disease. Normal male-pattern baldness follows a familial tendency to lose hair as men grow older, often beginning in the 20's and 30's and progressing to marked baldness in middle age. Baldness in almost all affected individuals follows a pattern, with a ring of hair left around the margin of the scalp.

There is no effective treatment for male-pattern baldness! In recent years, research workers have investigated the use of small amounts of male hormones taken orally or applied to the scalp. While some initial success seemed to follow this treatment, the absorption of the male hormones impaired normal testicular function, or perhaps set the stage for cancer of the prostate—too high a price to pay for vanity. Surgical methods involving transplantation of hair from actively growing areas change the appearance of those undergoing the procedure. I have always encouraged my balding patients to accept their familial hair distribution with equanimity, avoiding vain attempts to curl a few remaining strands over their enlarging bald spots.

Elderly women may suffer progressive thinning of the hair, but rarely, if ever, progress to the pattern baldness of the male. The cyclic use of estrogens, of benefit to women over 65 for many reasons, may help to arrest the condition, and thyroid hormone tablets and B_{12} injections have been used with favorable results in some individuals.

Another type of baldness is caused by disease; the appropriate treatment depends upon diagnosis of the specific illness. Ringworm or bacterial infection of the scalp can destroy small hair follicles, calling for prompt therapy of the local infection. Some emotionally disturbed persons habitually snatch out tiny clumps of hair, even during sleep, causing a patchy type of baldness. The appropriate treatment for this condition, called trichotillomania, is psychotherapy and a prescription for appropriate tranquilizers. Hair loss may be caused by the toxic effects of various chemicals such as heparin, huge quantities of vitamin A, and anticancer drugs such as nitrogen mustard or folic acid antagonists.

Alopecia areata is a fairly common condition, with rapid loss of hair in a patchy distribution; the cause is not known. Following the sudden loss, the hair regrows spontaneously in 80 per cent of cases, but only after a variable period of time. Finally, hair loss may be caused by a host of systemic illnesses, including such diverse disorders as advanced diabetes, lymphoma, lupus erythematosus, dermatomyositis, thyroid deficiency, and disorders of the pituitary gland.

VITILIGO

Vitiligo is a patchy loss of pigment from the skin, which appears unusually white and fails to tan. Consequently, vitiligo is less apparent in the winter and is more noticeable in the summer when the normal skin takes a tan. Vitiligo may be a distressing cosmetic problem in the Negro.

The cause of vitiligo is usually unknown, although a severe prolonged skin infection may occasionally be the culprit. Although the administration of psoralen compounds has been helpful in a few cases, vitiligo usually does not respond well to treatment. It is not a serious condition and does not predispose to cancer.

ATHLETE'S FOOT

Athlete's foot is a fungus infection, usually found between the toes, although severe cases may cover the sides and bottom of the foot. The fungus of athlete's foot is contagious, and the disease is usually contracted by walking on floors on which the fungus has been deposited. A common pattern of contagion is transmission to older household members from teenagers who have contracted athlete's foot in the locker room at school.

The symptoms of athlete's foot are severe itching, burning, and redness of the involved part of the foot, perhaps with clear drainage from small blisters. In prolonged cases, marked scaling and cracking of the feet may occur.

Athlete's foot is treated with creams and lotions that destroy the fungus and return the skin to its normal consistency. Tinactin cream applied locally to the athlete's foot three times a day is usually effective, and Vioform cream has been helpful in many cases. The doctor may prescribe ultraviolet light therapy. Desenex powder may be sprinkled in the socks and shoes before donning footwear; severe cases may require the use of griseofulvin tablets for from four to eight weeks. The afflicted person must avoid passing his fungus infection to other members of the family; walking barefoot in the shower or locker room is strictly forbidden. Since fungus infections grow luxuriantly in warm moist areas of the body, athlete's foot is prevented by using light, well-ventilated footwear and clean socks daily.

SKIN INFECTIONS

Older persons may be troubled by bacterial skin infections, caused by staphylococcus aureus, the notorious "staph" germ that now scoffs at penicillin therapy. The first bacterial invaders enter through a small scratch or inflamed hair follicle, soon multiplying to form a boil or furuncle. Once established, the infection discharges millions of bacteria onto the skin, and boils may form in nearby areas or spread to other members of the family.

Treatment of staphylococcal skin infections includes antibiotics by injection, tablets, or capsules. Many antibiotics have been found to be effective: erythromycin, Keflin, Cleocin, and the newer synthetic penicillins that resist inactivation. The local infection is soaked three or four times a day with a warm salt solution, either table salt or Epsom salts; I recommend one teaspoon of salt to one pint of warm water. After soaking for 30 minutes, an antibiotic such as Bacitracin ointment may be applied; if a pus pocket has formed, surgical drainage is needed.

The infected person and all other family members should take a thorough shower daily with plenty of soap and water. The bed clothes, linen, and underwear of the infected person should be boiled before washing and ironed after drying to kill all bacteria.

Because staphylococcal skin infections are more common in diabetics and persons devouring candy and cake, any victim of recurrent skin infections should be checked for possible diabetes.

Prevention of skin infections includes scrupulous personal cleanliness and daily changes of underwear. If a staphylococcal disease is present in the household, all skin infections, however minor, should be reported promptly to the doctor.

MONILIA

Moniliasis is a skin infection caused by a troublesome fungus called monilia, or candida, sometimes found in the bowel or vagina and which thrives in warm, moist skin folds. Infection is more common in diabetics, in elderly individuals who are weakened by disease, and in persons receiving prolonged antibiotic therapy, which destroys the normal intestinal bacteria, leaving the monilia free to multiply unchecked. Monilia may attack the mouth, the vagina, and skin folds under the arms, under the breasts, around the rectum, and between the legs. Monilia causes an intense itching and burning and a characteristic purple-red shiny inflammation of the skin. The main infection will entirely cover the involved area; at the edges small islands of disease will be seen invading normal skin. Inasmuch as monilia resists all over-the-counter drugstore remedies, the sufferer who suspects monilia should consult a physician. The infection will respond promptly to proper diagnosis and appropriate local therapy. Mycostatin, available as a cream, an oral suspension, and in vaginal tablets, is highly effective against this yeast infection; in stubborn cases, Mycostatin tablets may be taken by mouth to subdue monilia growth in the large intestine. Treatment should be continued for at least five days after the infection has apparently been cured to prevent the occasional lingering organism from reestablishing itself.

CONTACT RASHES

Contact rashes occur when an irritant substance causes itching, burning, redness, and swelling, usually assuming the shape of the object in contact with the skin. The possible causes of contact rash are legion. A nickel-plated wristwatch and band on the skin of a susceptible individual will leave a beefy rash encircling the wrist. I have examined young men carrying leaking cigarette lighters in their trouser pockets who show a perfect rectangular patch conforming to the shape of the lighter. Housewives who are intolerant of detergents can develop a violent skin reaction limited to the hands. Poison ivy, which may be spread by touching or by inhalation of fumes from the burning leaves, is really a contact rash. Cosmetics, including toothpaste, nail polish, and perfumes, are common sources of contact allergy. Hat bands may cause an inflamed ring around the scalp and forehead, and an irritated underarm may be a contact reaction to a deodorant. Household cleansers, turpentine, plastic, varnishes, dye, and soaps may all cause a contact skin rash of the hands. Young persons wearing leather thong sandals from India have suffered a skin rash with a characteristic pattern of the feet, caused by a chemical used in tanning the leather.

Treatment of the contact rash is identification and removal of the irritant. The nickel-plated watch band must be discarded in favor of a leather or cloth band, and strong household detergent must be replaced by milder soaps, perhaps handled through rubber gloves. Fortunately, most pharmacies now carry a full line of hypoallergenic cosmetics.

Along with the elimination of the causative product, the contact rash may be treated with a cortisone cream, such as one-quarter or one-half per cent hydrocortisone cream, which gives prompt relief from irritation and itching. In severe reactions, cortisone may be given by tablets or injection with even faster relief. Prevention of the contact rash requires only keeping a safe distance from the irritating object or substance.

MOLES

Moles begin at various ages, are often present at birth, and increase in frequency during later years. Although cosmetically unattractive, moles are of little importance except for those few that become cancerous. Unfortunately, however, the cancer arising from moles, called malignant melanoma, is a highly lethal tumor. In an effort to decide which moles should be removed for analysis, let us consider some generalities that have guided doctors through the years:

All moles that enlarge or change shape should be removed.

All moles that show a halo of pigment growing around the main mole should be removed.

Remove all moles subject to frequent irritation, including those on the collar line, the bra line, the belt line, and on the palms of the hands or soles of the feet.

Any mole that shows bleeding, irritation, or pain should be removed.

Moles with stiff coarse hairs emerging from them are almost never malignant.

The decision to remove a mole rests with the physician. All worrisome moles should be brought to your doctor's attention; if suspicious, they will be excised and sent for analysis in the laboratory.

KERATOSES

Keratoses are growths occurring in aging skin, usually in areas that have been exposed to solar radiation during decades of working in the sun. On the East Coast, the condition is called "sailor's skin;" Midwesterners call the same condition "farmer's skin." Keratoses are raised dry scaling growths that have been described as similar to a drop of dirty candle wax on the skin, with a "stuck on" appearance and seeming ready to drop off. However, they do not drop off, and ill-advised attempts at home removal will be punished by brisk bleeding.

Since a skin cancer sometimes masquerades as a keratosis, any previously harmless growth that shows ulceration or recurrent bleeding should be promptly removed. Otherwise, these multiple lesions require surgery only for cosmetic reasons.

SKIN CANCER

Skin cancer is properly called basal or squamous cell carcinoma of the skin and is a different tumor from that arising in moles. The tumor begins as a sore ulcerated bleeding area in the skin usually surrounded by a raised rolled edge, perhaps occurring on any area of the body, but most commonly on such exposed areas as the face, arms, and neck. Most skin cancers grow very slowly and are totally curable if recognized and removed within a reasonable period of time. Since skin cancers usually do not spread, but destroy tissue by local invasion of nearby organs, death from skin cancer can occur only from continued neglect.

All ulcerated bleeding chronic sores should be examined by the family physician, who will decide whether removal is necessary. Surgically removed specimens should be sent to the laboratory to determine the nature of the growth and verify completeness of removal.

General rules of skin care for the senior citizen:

Avoid excessive exposure to the sun—it can set the stage for keratoses and skin cancer.

Avoid harsh detergents. Even excessive handwashing may be irritating.

Bathe daily, followed by a change of underwear.

Avoid such chemicals as kerosene, turpentine, and acetone.

Don't pick, squeeze, or cut skin lesions.

Treat all skin infection promptly.

Have any and all suspicious sores or growths examined by the doctor.

The Bones and Joints After 65

The human body . . . indeed is like a ship; its bones being the stiff-standing rigging, and the sinews the small running ropes, that manage all the motions.
HERMAN MELVILLE
(1819-1891)

THE CHANGES OF AGING

Aging brings a gradual weakening of the bones and joints that can give rise to disease. Bones consist of a protein framework made firm by the presence of calcium and phosphorus crystals, and aging bone becomes both weak and brittle. Since the soft bones in the vertebrae of the spinal column show slight compression from carrying the weight of the body, with age there may be some loss in height. Weakened bones, deficient in calcium and phosphorus, may show an increased suscepti-bility to fractures.

The joints, hinges wherever two bones meet, are vitally important for normal function of the limbs. The end of the bone forming the joint is normally cushioned by a thin layer of cartilage, which begins to fragment with advancing age. The youthful joint is restricted in its motion by ligaments that hold the bones in place, but these ligaments stretch as time takes its toll. The moving joints are lubricated by fluid within them; with age, diminished secretion of this fluid causes dryness of the joints. Dry crumbling joints, supported by weakened ligaments, set the stage for the diseases discussed in this chapter.

FOOT PROBLEMS

Problems of the feet after 65 include bunions, ingrown toenails, corns, and calluses. The bunion, a good example of the type of joint disorder that begins during the middle years and becomes troublesome after 65, is a partial dislocation of the first joint of the big toe. With age, the protective cartilage in the joint fragments, and the secretions become dry, causing pain; weakened ligaments supporting the joint allow the big toe to be pushed to the side by tight shoes, and the base of the big toe is displaced toward the middle (see Figure 21).

Bunions are caused by improperly fitted footwear; the worst offenders are tight pointed toes that cramp the big toe. Once present, bunions respond best to surgical correction of the deformed joint. Some devices that return the toe to its proper position have had limited success. However, therapy is doomed to failure if the individual continues to wear improperly fitted shoes.

Ingrown toenail, although tending to run in families, is often aggravated by ill-fitting shoes or tight stockings. Improper cutting of

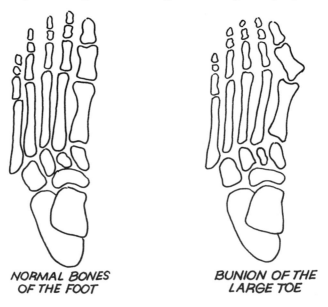

NORMAL BONES
OF THE FOOT

BUNION OF THE
LARGE TOE

Fig. 21. The Human Foot

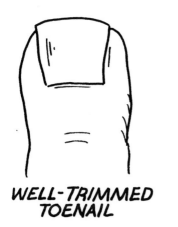

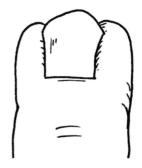

WELL-TRIMMED TOENAIL

INCORRECTLY CUT TOENAIL

Fig. 22. Trimming the Toenails

the toenails, with the nails carefully rounded like fingernails, allows the nail margin to dig into tender skin. The nail that has grown into the surrounding tissue causes pain, swelling, redness, and perhaps infection, sometimes with the formation of pus.

Initially, the ingrown toenail is treated with warm salt water soaks to subdue inflammation and infection, followed by the application of an antibiotic ointment if infection is present. The patient is advised to cut the toenails straight across to minimize their digging into the tissues (see Figure 22). In cases that are not infected, a wad of cotton is placed under the nail to elevate it out of the tissue (see Figure 23); a few drops

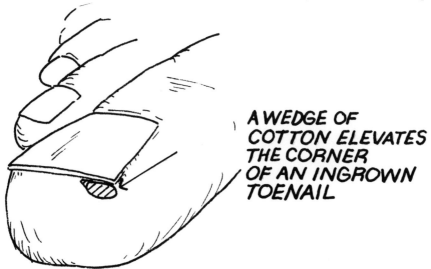

A WEDGE OF COTTON ELEVATES THE CORNER OF AN INGROWN TOENAIL

Fig. 23. The Avoidance of Ingrown Toenails

of flexible collodion placed on the cotton will hold it in place for several weeks. Severely ingrown nails may require surgery, with removal of all or part of the nail and the nearby overgrowing tissue.

Corns and calluses are a build-up of the outer scaling layer of the skin that pushes into the feet when walking, like a pebble in the shoe. Most corns and calluses are caused by improperly fitted footwear rubbing on the foot; the skin responds by building up protective hard tissue. Corns and calluses may also be caused by an abnormal bone in the foot, which may require surgery for correction.

PROPER SHOES

Painful feet, often the penalty for wearing improper footwear, can be disabling. An otherwise vigorous 74-year-old lady shunned shopping trips or walks in the park because of painful swollen feet. For years she attributed this disability to her age: "Oh my! If only I were 30 again." Upon reconsideration, however, Mrs. Jenkins realized that her feet were no older than the rest of her body.

Examination of her feet showed mild swelling, with bulging bunions and colossal calluses at pressure points. Her pointed-toe shoes were stretched like old garters and showed uneven wear of the soles. Her good sense overcome by vanity, the lady had for many years been squeezing her size 8C feet into size 7-1/2B shoes and now was suffering the consequences.

This patient was advised to donate all her ill-fitting footwear to her favorite charity and purchase new shoes in her proper size under the watchful eye of a salesman trained in the latest methods of fitting shoes. She was instructed to select the wider toes that now have become fashionable. High heels were forbidden, and she was advised to select strong soles so that walking would be a pleasure again.

When examined one month later, my patient reported that she was scarcely aware of her feet. Her bunions were still present, but gave her much less discomfort. Corns and calluses were beginning to soften and were causing a great deal less trouble. Most important, the lady was able to enjoy long walks with her grandchildren, a pleasure not possible several months before.

GANGLION OF THE WRIST

The ganglion, which may occur at any age, is a swelling of the wrist or occasionally the ankle. The tendons that connect muscles to bone lie within a sheath that allows easy movement, thanks to a thick lubricating fluid. With minor injuries, the tendon sheath of the wrist or ankle may swell, forming a fluid-filled sac the size of a pea or a marble. Ganglions are initially somewhat tender, although severe pain is uncommon.

Ganglion of the wrist is best treated by "observation," although a number of treatment methods have been advocated during the colorful history of medicine. The oldest known therapy was to place the offending wrist across the corner of the dining room table and strike it with the family Bible, breaking the ganglion and often the wrist as well. Some ganglia are removed surgically, but the operation may be followed by recurrence within six months. The fluid in large ganglia may be removed in the doctor's office with a needle and syringe; while this method of treatment may be initially successful, within a week many ganglia will fill again. If allowed to remain, most ganglia will form scar tissue, reduce in size, and present no further problems.

BURSITIS

A bursa is a thin sac located where skin passes over a bony prominence and contains a lubricating fluid that allows smooth movement of the bones beneath the skin. Bursae are present in the shoulder, elbow, knee, and other areas. Bursitis is an inflammation of the bursa, causing swelling, redness, pain, and often enlargement following an accumulation of fluid.

Bursitis is treated with cold applications (although heat is sometimes prescribed), antibiotics if infection is present, and aspiration with a needle and syringe if the sac is swollen with fluid. Sometimes following needle removal of fluid, a cortisone compound is injected directly into the bursa; alternatively, cortisone tablets are given by mouth. Bursitis often responds slowly to treatment, and recurrence at a later time is not uncommon.

Bursitis, often striking without warning or apparent cause, cannot always be prevented, but the following may help.

Healthful prophylactic measures include:

Avoid trauma to joints.

Shun unaccustomed repetitive exercise such as bowling, sawing lumber, chopping wood, and vigorous calisthenics.

Exercise is good, but begin gradually or pay the penalty.

GOUT

Gout is the accumulation in joints of crystals of uric acid, a normal breakdown product of protein metabolism. Gout sufferers are unable to excrete uric acid properly; this concentrates in the bloodstream, causing crystals to be deposited in the joints and giving rise to pain, heat, redness, and swelling.

The most commonly involved area is the first joint of the large toe. In the past, gout was considered a disease of wealthy English noblemen, probably because only the affluent could afford the high living to which gout was formerly attributed. In the United States, where almost everyone eats a diet high in protein, gout is becoming a common problem.

The treatment of gout has two phases: the reduction of the prevailing high blood level of uric acid and relief of the acute attack of gout. The latter is treated with Butazolidin, colchicine, Indocin, and, on rare occasions, cortisone. Colchicine, taken one tablet every two hours, will successfully relieve only gout and is therefore a useful diagnostic test. Since cortisone, Butazolidin, and Indocin are useful in both acute gout and acute arthritis, their success in therapy is not of diagnostic value.

Once the acute attack of gout has subsided, long-term therapy to prevent future attacks must be planned. The memory of the excruciating pain of the gout attack lingers, and the physician has little difficulty in enlisting the patient's cooperation. The doctor usually prescribes a daily dose of medication, either Benemid or Zyloprim, to reduce the uric acid in the bloodstream. The patient should eat a well-balanced diet, avoiding beer, liver, kidneys, sweetbreads, meat extracts, turkey, shellfish, herring, sardines, and anchovies. The breakdown products of these foods boost the blood uric acid and may lead to an attack of gout. Drinking plenty of water helps prevent the formation of uric acid crystals in the kidneys. Since acute attacks of gout may occur when one is run-down, the patient should maintain good health habits, with plenty of rest and exercise.

You can help prevent gout by:

Keeping your weight down.

Avoiding the specific foods mentioned above.

Taking six glasses of water each day to dissolve uric acid crystals in the urine.

Staying out of cold damp places.

Checking with your doctor about the possibility that any new medication, such as a diuretic, may lead to a gout attack.

RHEUMATOID ARTHRITIS

Rheumatoid arthritis is the crippling type of joint disease that usually attacks young adults, although occasionally attacks will begin after 65. The exact cause of rheumatoid arthritis is not known. The disease presents an inflammation in the lining cells of the joints, with heat, swelling, and redness of all involved joints, plus malaise and perhaps fever. Rheumatoid arthritis is a seesaw disease, having unpredictable ups and downs, although there may be flare-ups at the time of colds, flu, or emotional turmoil.

Damp cold weather makes rheumatoid arthritis worse. As John W. Strutt remarked in a letter, "I cannot conceive why we who are composed of over 90 percent water should suffer from rheumatism with a slight rise in the humidity of the atmosphere."

Five different medications make up the defense against rheumatoid arthritis. Salicylates such as aspirin are the backbone of the treatment, and all sufferers whose stomachs can tolerate the dosage should take 8 to 12 five-grain aspirin tablets daily. Indocin, the next most commonly used drug for arthritis, is safe and is effective even in long-term use. Butazolidin, although not safe for prolonged use, is often beneficial when given in 10- to 14-day courses of therapy. Cortisone, also not safe for long-term use, can afford blessed relief when taken for a few days or weeks. Injections of gold salts such as Solganal are used for resistant cases.

Proper treatment of rheumatoid arthritis includes daily physical therapy with such active or passive exercises as the condition permits. Local applications of heat to the joints, including hot packs, heating pads, and paraffin baths for the hands are soothing. Careful attention to proper diet with vitamins is essential, and obese patients must shed excess pounds. With proper medication, exercise, and diet, the rheumatoid arthritis patient has the best chance of avoiding the severe crippling once the hallmark of the disease.

OSTEOARTHRITIS

Osteoarthritis is the gradual joint degeneration of age as the tissues become dry, as the protective cartilage disintegrates, and as brittle bone ends rub against each other painfully. The patient may first notice aching enlargements of the last joint of the fingers called Heberden's nodes (see Figure 24). Overweight persons will feel pain and a grating sensation in the knees; in fact, osteoarthritis may involve any joint of the body, including the spine.

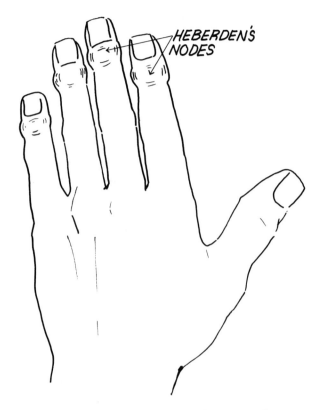

Fig. 24. Osteoarthritis of the Hand

Osteoarthritis is treated with medication to relieve the pain and inflammation, notably aspirin and Indocin, although Butazolidin and cortisone, taken in short courses, are sometimes useful. The burden of excess fat is shed to ease aching knees, and inflamed joints are treated by the application of heat for half an hour four times a day. Repair of the bones may be enhanced by taking a hormone such as Winstrol or Dianabol to increase protein build-up in the bone.

Osteoarthritis, like rheumatoid arthritis, is more painful in cold damp temperate zones than in warmer climates and is often the motivating factor in the decision to spend the golden years in Florida, Arizona, or Southern California.

Although the inevitable wear and tear of osteoarthritis may not be preventable, *the following rules will minimize discomfort and disability:*

Maintain your ideal weight.

Avoid cold damp areas.

Get plenty of rest.

Guard against injury to joints.

Exercise regularly.

Eat a nutritious diet.

CHRONIC BACKACHE

"Doctor, my back aches day and night; I can't even bend to tie my shoes." Improper habits of sitting, standing, and working cause most chronic backaches. The human body is structurally engineered to walk on all fours, and our impertinence in walking on our hind limbs predisposes us to chronic low backache. Obesity results in a swayback posture to compensate for the protuberant abdomen, and "television slouch" can be a cause of low back discomfort. Habitual bending from the waist to perform such household tasks as making the bed or lifting an infant; wearing high heels; sitting on chairs without proper back support; and failure to obtain adequate rest—all are factors in chronic backache.

The treatment of this condition begins by correcting harmful habits of standing, sitting, bending, and sleeping. The housewife who spends hours standing at her kitchen counter should place one foot on a footrest to lock the hips and relieve the low back strain. When one sits in a chair, the feet should be elevated on a hassock so that the knees are higher than the hips, relieving strain on the low back. Bending from the waist is strictly forbidden. A good firm mattress is essential for proper rest of the back. Simple pain killers such as aspirin may be prescribed for temporary relief of pain, and a heating pad may be helpful but, with correction of improper habits of posture, these measures should no longer be necessary.

Here are the rules to prevent backache:

Never bend from the waist when lifting.

Don't try to lift a heavy weight without help.

Avoid high-heel shoes.

Sleep on a firm mattress.

Walk tall. Don't slouch.

Avoid prolonged standing.

SCIATICA

Sciatica is a severe low back pain that radiates down one leg. There is an inflammation of the sciatic nerve, which arises in the spine and passes through the pelvis on its way down the back of the leg. The pain originates in the spine, with pressure on the root of the sciatic nerve caused by an arthritic bone spur or a slipped disc. The pain is severe and often constant. The patient will frequently notice a numb, heavy feeling in the leg; neurological examination by the doctor may reveal loss of motion, impaired sensation of pain, and sometimes shrinkage of muscle in the leg.

Sciatica is a more serious condition than chronic backache, and bed rest for at least seven to ten days will be required to reduce inflammation of the nerve. Various methods of applying heat, including hot packs, ultrasound therapy, and diathermy, have been used. Analgesics such as aspirin, Darvon, or Zactirin help relieve the pain. I have found cortisone by injection or in tablet form useful in some cases of sciatic nerve inflammation although severe cases involving a slipped disc in the spine will often require surgery.

FRACTURES

Fractures are broken bones, more common in the elderly because bones deficient in calcium become brittle. Following a fall, any painful bone should be X-rayed for possible fracture. Since older persons with broken bones may not feel the acute pain evident in younger people, the physician must always be alert to the possibility of a fracture.

Fractures in persons over 65 present the problem of the need for a cast or splint, with the additional worry that prolonged immobilization may cause joint stiffening. The skill of a watchmaker and the judgment of a prime minister are necessary in the treatment of any fracture in the older person. Because of such complicating problems as arthritis, a mild deformity that would be corrected surgically in a younger person must often be accepted.

Fracture of the hip is the Waterloo of the senior citizen. A fall on a scatter rug, a misstep on a slippery floor, or a fast turn with the foot planted can snap the hipbone (see Figure 25). The fractured hip will cause pain, but does not always make walking impossible.

X rays will reveal the fracture of the hip; the exact method of treatment will depend upon the nature and location of the fracture. While some elderly bedfast patients are treated without surgery, operative repair of the fractured hip, with a wide choice of pins and nails, is recommended for most persons capable of rehabilitation.

Physical therapy following surgery is the next step in the long road to recovery. Active and passive exercises of the hip and progressive

Fig. 25. Fracture of the Hip

activity lead to full ambulation. After the hospital stay, a two- to six-week period of continued therapy in a nursing home may be beneficial.

With prompt surgery and proper physical therapy, the older person who is in good general health and enjoys mental alertness should make an excellent recovery, with restoration of walking within several months.

CANCER OF THE BONE

Cancer of the bone may arise within the bone itself or spread from another area. Cancer originating in the bone, causing pain and swelling at the local site, is usually visible on X-ray examination. The decision as to the type of treatment, whether surgery or irradiation, will be determined by the location and size of the tumor.

Cancer that has originated in another area and spread to the bone is more common and often follows cancer of the breast, prostate, stomach, pancreas, and large intestine. The secondary bone tumor, called metastatic, first makes itself known by severe pain, often linked with a fracture caused by a very minor injury.

X rays show the cancer in the bone, and further tests may disclose unsuspected cancer lurking in other areas. A search should be made for the primary source of the cancer, since proper therapy depends upon the nature of the original tumor.

Cancer of the bone often causes severe pain, but fortunately the discomfort will usually respond favorably to X-ray therapy. Resistant cases may be eased by chemical therapy such as nitrogen mustard, but surgery has little place in the treatment of such cancers. While the spread of cancer from another site to the bone represents an incurable disease, a great deal can be done to relieve pain and prolong life.

Diseases
of the Pancreas
After 65

*Man may be the captain of his fate, but he is
also the victim of his blood sugar.*
WILFRID G. OAKLEY
Transactions of the Medical
Society of London, 78:16 (1962)

THE CHANGES OF AGING

The pancreas, a three-inch-long narrow gland lying in the abdominal cavity, has two functions: the secretion of enzymes to aid in digestion and the production of insulin, which is important in the metabolism of sugar. Fat and scar tissue replace normal cells in the aging pancreas, decreasing the enzymes released into the intestinal tract and sometimes causing impaired digestion of fats, proteins, and carbohydrates. Although there may be mild symptoms of indigestion and flatulence, ebbing pancreatic enzymes usually present no serious problem to the older person.

Deficient production of insulin by the aging pancreas is a more troublesome problem. As the pancreas grows older, the cells producing insulin wear out, and insufficient insulin is produced. Thus begins diabetes.

DIABETES MELLITUS

Diabetes is one of the oldest diseases known to mankind. Egyptian writings 3500 years old describe this disorder; the ancient Greeks first used the term diabetes, which means "siphon," referring to a common symptom of uncontrolled diabetes: frequent urination. Later, physicians discovered that the urine tasted sweet, owing to the presence of sugar in the urine, and the Latin word *mellitus,* meaning "honey," was added. Until the 20th century, the finding of sugar in the urine was usually a death sentence. There was no treatment available for diabetes until 1921, when the Canadian physicians Frederick G. Banting and Charles W. Best discovered insulin, a hormone produced in the pancreas that allows normal metabolism of carbohydrates.

Insulin transports carbohydrates from the bloodstream into the cells of the body. Since the diabetic lacks enough insulin, carbohydrates are unable to enter the body cells and therefore accumulate in the blood. With excessive sugar in the blood and a sugar shortage in the cells, two changes lead to acid build-up in the body. First, large quantities of sugar in the bloodstream are passed in the urine. Since sugar attracts water, the kidney excretes large quantities of water along with the sugar, leaving the body dehydrated and with an increased concentration of acid products in the bloodstream. Second, the cells, lacking sugar for energy, break down fats and protein for this use. The metabolic waste products of protein and fat breakdown are acids, and these are released into the blood, adding to the acidity of the body.

Uncontrolled diabetes causes dehydration because of excess urine passage and accumulation of acid in the bloodstream. Impaired consciousness, called diabetic coma, may occur. The patient will show heavy deep breathing as the body tries to remove acid as carbon dioxide from the lungs.

The first attack of diabetes may occur during a cold, flu, surgical operation, or other stressful situation. Diabetes may lurk in hiding for many years, rising to the surface when illness weakens the body's defenses.

The physician detects diabetes by testing the blood and urine for sugar; often a blood specimen is drawn following a test meal containing a known amount of sugar. The normal fasting blood sugar is approximately 100 milligrams; blood sugar values over 140 milligrams usually represent diabetes.

Most diabetics diagnosed after 65 can be controlled with diet, perhaps supplemented by pills. Orinase, the product most widely used in the United States today, is a safe effective compound that has proved useful for control of mild diabetes. Orinase tablets are taken one to four times daily; if the diabetes is not too severe, there should be a smooth return of blood sugar to normal limits. Diabinese, Dymelor, and Tolinase are other oral medications often prescribed for senior diabetics. A compound called DBI comes in a time-disintegration capsule that can have a stabilizing effect on blood sugar and is useful in overweight diabetics.

A few diabetics beginning after age 65 will require insulin. Regular insulin, also called crystalline insulin, is a pure form having a six-hour duration of action. Regular insulin is used when a rapid response is necessary in surgery, severe illness, and coma. Most diabetics, however, will achieve day-by-day balance by using the long-acting insulins, Lente and NPH. These have a 24-hour duration of action, and one injection in the morning allows coverage through the day, reaching a peak of activity about suppertime and gradually falling off during the night. Most diabetics can be stablized on a single morning dose of NPH or Lente insulin.

Diabetics show a higher incidence of obesity, heart attacks, and hypertension than the normal population, and gangrene of the feet following advanced arteriosclerosis of the leg arteries is not uncommon. Diabetics suffer skin and foot infections more frequently than normal persons; urinary infections are common, probably because of the presence of sugar in the urine; and weakness of the nerves of the legs is often seen in diabetes of long standing. An important aspect of the treatment of diabetes mellitus is anticipation and prevention of these complications. The diabetic must pay strict attention to care of the feet. Toenails must be cut straight across and with extreme care (see Figure 22). Shoes must be carefully fitted to avoid pressure on the toes or heels that might cause sores, and any foot infection, however minor, should be brought to the attention of the physician. Urinary infections should receive prompt and prolonged treatment, and catheterization should be avoided in diabetics if at all possible. The diabetic must receive scrupulous skin care with aggressive therapy of all minor skin infections, minimize his intake of fats and cholesterol to prevent arteriosclerosis, and maintain good health habits with adequate rest and exercise.

Before the life-saving discovery of insulin, diet was the only treatment available to diabetics. Each gram of food was carefully calculated, weighed, and recorded before it was consumed—taking all the fun out of mealtime. As doctors learned more about diabetes and as insulin and other drugs became available, extremely strict dietary control became less important. The diabetic's personal physician will prescribe a meal plan, and it is important that the diabetic understand the dual goals of the diet: to attain the ideal weight and to minimize the carbohydrates the body must metabolize.

Diabetes is linked to obesity. Many persons who have become diabetic at age 40 or 50 would have delayed the onset of the disease for several decades had they entered middle age without a flabby spare tire and protruding paunch. All diabetics should determine the ideal weight for their height and reduce their caloric intake accordingly. Because diabetes is a deficiency of carbohydrate metabolism and because carbohydrates are the body's source of energy, the diabetic diet controls the amount of carbohydrates that the body must metabolize.

The diabetic diet will contain the appropriate number of calories for the patient's age, perhaps 1,500 or 2,000 calories, and will stress the importance of protein, vegetables, and fresh fruit. There will be a minimal intake of bread, potatoes, and dairy products, while sugar, cakes, pies, and candies are strictly forbidden. Although most mild diabetics need only adopt the liberal diet outlined above, the severe diabetic must follow a strict dietary prescription regulated by his personal physician.

Can diabetes be prevented? Although a hereditary disease, the onset of diabetes can be delayed many years by appropriate measures. Persons with diabetes in the family, and indeed all adults, should avoid excessive intake of sweets and pastry, and ideal weight should be maintained. Since it is desirable to detect diabetes on routine examination rather than by the occurrence of diabetic coma in the midst of a flu attack, the person over 65, and indeed all adults, should have a yearly physical examination that includes a blood sugar test.

PANCREATITIS

Pancreatitis is an inflammation of the pancreas, more common in men than in women, and often associated with alcoholism, gallstones, peptic ulcer, or a direct blow to the abdomen.

The normal pancreas secretes digestive enzymes that flow through a narrow tube to the small intestine. When pancreatitis blocks this normal flow, the trapped enzymes begin to digest the cells of the pancreas itself. This self-destruction causes lancinating pain in the middle abdomen, tenderness upon palpation, restlessness, and often shock. The physician will diagnose pancreatitis by careful history, physical examination, and laboratory measurement of the pancreatic enzymes: amylase and lipase. Acute pancreatitis may be treated with antispasmodics to reduce pancreatic secretion, intravenous fluids to minimize the need for pancreatic enzymes, analgesics if necessary for pain, and supplementary vitamins to help maintain nutrition.

Because pancreatitis is related to alcoholism, gallstones, and peptic ulcer, its prevention calls for relief of these predisposing conditions.

HYPOGLYCEMIA

Hypoglycemia means low blood sugar. It may occur in a diabetic who receives too much insulin, in a busy executive who skips meals, or in a victim of functional hypoglycemia—an uncommon condition in which the body reacts to eating carbohydrates by producing too much insulin, plummeting the blood sugar to dangerously low levels. The symptoms of low blood sugar, whatever the cause, are dizziness, sweating, and a jittery feeling of impending danger. If allowed to progress, the patient may become unconscious, and convulsions sometimes occur.

The immediate treatment of hypoglycemia is to boost the level of sugar in the bloodstream by oral feedings or injections of glucose. If awake, the patient is given ginger ale or orange juice laced with sugar. Following relief of the acute symptoms, the patient should eat a meal so that the blood sugar will stay up. If unconscious, the patient is given Glucagon, an injectable substance that boosts blood sugar and that should be kept in the homes of all persons who take insulin for diabetes. Glucagon is easily mixed and injected safely by any family member, into virtually any part of the body, following the doctor's instructions.

Functional hypoglycemia, an overreaction to carbohydrates, is treated with a special diet similar to the diabetic diet, high in proteins, vegetables, and fresh fruits and low in carbohydrates. It is paradoxical that, while sweets may relieve the temporary symptoms of functional hypoglycemia, they actually bring on a more severe attack. Since functional hypoglycemia is a disorder of carbohydrate metabolism, many younger persons with this disability will, in later years, become diabetic.

CANCER OF THE PANCREAS

Cancer of the pancreas is an insidious and highly malignant tumor, rarely detected until it has advanced to an incurable stage. The first clue to pancreatic carcinoma may be a dull nagging ache in the upper abdomen, coupled with mild indigestion. Back pain and weight loss are late symptoms, usually accompanying advanced disease that has already invaded the liver and bone.

Carcinoma of the pancreas is treated with surgical removal whenever possible. Since this involves an extensive operation with a prolonged recovery period, the surgeon must consider whether the possible benefits justify the heroic procedure. Back pain caused by spread of the cancer to the bones of the spine eases following radiation therapy. Pain killers such as Darvon or codeine are given for discomfort, and Demerol or morphine is often used for more severe pain. The outlook for the victim of cancer of the pancreas is dismal, and the life expectancy from the time of diagnosis will be about 9 to 12 months.

Thyroid Problems in the Senior Citizen

New York, The Nation's Thyroid Gland.
CHRISTOPHER MORLEY
(1890-1957)

THE CHANGES OF AGING

The thyroid gland, lying in the neck just above the chest, manufactures thyroid hormone, which is important in maintaining the energy level of the body. Persons with normal amounts of thyroid hormone feel robust and vigorous, have a healthy appetite, and are able to perform a day's work without undue fatigue; with excessive thyroid, however, there is an abnormally rapid metabolism, and body tissues are burned for energy, causing tiredness and weight loss.

The thyroid, however, becomes smaller and produces less hormone as it ages. In many cases, the mild thyroid slowdown is beneficial, because the aging heart and blood vessels might not withstand the metabolic strain of a vigorous 20-year-old's activity. Usually the mild slowdown in production of thyroid hormone is not perceptible and does not present a medical problem. The changes of the thyroid gland are part of the normal aging process, and the elderly person should not be given thyroid hormone to stimulate him unless a clear-cut thyroid deficiency can be demonstrated by laboratory testing.

GOITER

A goiter is an enlarged thyroid. The thyroid may enlarge as the body attempts to make up for deficient thyroid production; the enlargement may be unrelated to function; or there may be a growth present in the gland. With thyroid hormone deficiency, there is enlargement of the existing thyroid cells as the gland attempts to compensate for the deficiency by increased production of hormone, causing enlargement of the gland in the neck.

The enlarging thyroid gland is visible to the patient and to the casual observer (see Figure 26). If it is sufficiently enlarged, there may be pressure on the trachea (windpipe), causing shortness of breath; with dramatic enlargement, there may be difficulty in swallowing. If the goiter is caused by thyroid deficiency, the symptoms of hypothyroidism—cold feet, brittle hair, weight gain, and sluggishness—may be present.

The treatment of goiter associated with a thyroid hormone deficiency is the administration of thyroid extract or perhaps one of the synthetic thyroid hormones, such as Synthroid or Cytomel. As the thyroid cells are no longer called upon to work overtime, the gland should shrink back to normal size gradually.

Fig. 26. Thyroid Goiter

OVERACTIVE THYROID

The overactive thyroid, resulting in hyperthyroidism, produces colossal quantities of thyroid hormone that cause increased metabolism with a rapid pulse, weight loss, a jittery feeling, and sleeplessness. The blood pressure may be elevated. The fingertips will be warm to the touch, in contrast to the cold clammy hands of the nervous individual. The victim of an overactive thyroid may have a voracious appetite, but lose weight. The thyroid gland in the neck may be enlarged or may be of normal size, and in some cases bulging eyes will be a prominent symptom.

Overactive thyroid is treated with surgery, medication, or administration of radioactive iodine, all methods of treatment having as their goal a reduction in the amount of thyroid hormone produced. Surgical removal of part of the thyroid is performed on younger persons, particularly women of childbearing age, who should not be given radioactive material. Antithyroid medication such as propylthiouracil may be given to reduce thyroid function; the medication must be taken daily, and dosage adjustments will be made from time to time. The favored treatment for the senior citizen with hyperthyroidism is radioactive iodine (RAI). The RAI is plucked from the blood by the thyroid gland, concentrating the radioactivity in the thyroid cells. Careful calculation of the dosage can allow the destruction of exactly the right number of cells to achieve middle-of-the-road thyroid hormone production.

UNDERACTIVE THYROID

"Doctor, I feel tired all the time and my weight keeps going up." Underactivity of the thyroid, called hypothyroidism, causes a stingy production of thyroid hormone, with mental sluggishness, coarse hair, swelling of the lower legs and ankles, constipation, and puffiness of the face. Extreme obesity may be present, and in severe cases mental deterioration may occur. Many cases of underactive thyroid occur in persons over 65 who have undergone partial thyroid removal or radioactive iodine therapy for hyperthyroidism in years past. Because the gland will attempt to increase production of thyroid hormone, a noticeable thyroid enlargement, or goiter, may be present.

Hypothyroidism is treated by the administration of thyroid hormone; most cases require 1 to 3 grains of thyroid extract daily or the equivalent dose of synthetic thyroid hormone. Although maximum improvement may not be seen for from four to six weeks, the response to thyroid medication should then be dramatic. With appropriate thyroid replacement, the patient should become more alert and show a remarkable change in appearance. All elderly patients who have undergone partial removal of the thyroid in their earlier years are on the suspect list for the insidious onset of underactive thyroid.

CANCER OF THE THYROID

Cancer is first noted as a lump in the thyroid gland by the doctor upon physical examination or by the patient when buttoning a shirt or dress. Of all lumps found in the thyroid, probably about 10 per cent will turn out to be cancer, and all thyroid lumps should be reported to the physician for evaluation.

Upon discovering a lump in the thyroid, the doctor will order a thyroid scan to determine whether the lump contains normal thyroid cells or tissue that may be cancer. A tiny amount of radioactive-tagged substance is administered to be picked up by the thyroid cells, and a machine similar to a Geiger counter draws a graphic picture of the uptake of the radioactive substance by the thyroid gland. The presence of a normal uptake by a questionable lump shows that normal thyroid tissue is present, but a scanty uptake of radioactive material by a lump shouts "Cancer!" to the doctor. All questionable lumps will be removed by the surgeon for diagnosis.

Fortunately, carcinoma of the thyroid is usually a very slow-growing cancer, and there are many recorded cases of thyroid cancer victims living two decades or more. In order to achieve the best chance of cure, all lumps in the thyroid should be promptly reported to the physician for accurate diagnosis.

Urinary Problems
of the
Senior Citizen

FALSTAFF: What says the doctor to my water?
PAGE: He said, sir, the water itself was
a good healthy water; but, for the party that
owed it, he might have more diseases
than he knew for.

WILLIAM SHAKESPEARE
(1564-1616)
Henry IV, Part II

THE CHANGES OF AGING

Blood passing through the kidneys is filtered to remove waste products. Waste-containing urine flows from the kidneys through the ureters to the bladder and, after brief storage there, is passed from the bladder through the urethra (see Figure 27). Arteriosclerosis of the blood vessels to the kidneys causes deterioration of the cells, with less blood presented to the kidney for filtration, and there is a gradual build-up of wastes in the blood. With advancing age, the bladder wall sometimes sags, stretching to hold larger volumes of urine, and there may be a small amount of residual urine in the bladder after urination.

BLADDER INFECTION

As men draw near the common goal
Can anything be sadder
Than he who, master of his soul,
Is servant to his bladder.
The Speculum, 1938

Infection of the bladder, with bacteria and pus in the urine, causes painful burning upon urination, frequent passage of urine, and fitful sleep as one is forced to arise at night to pass urine. A bladder infection will often cause fever, along with cloudy urine emitting a foul odor. Bladder infection is more common in women than men because the bladder is close to the vagina, and bacteria, normal inhabitants of the vagina, journey up the short urethra to the bladder. Bladder infection strikes men when an enlarged prostate blocks complete emptying of the bladder and bacteria find a happy home in the residual urine. Because the bacteria thrive on the increased sugar in diabetic urine, bladder infections are more common in diabetics than in normal persons.

Bladder infections are treated with antibacterial preparations. Sulfonamides are the traditional therapy for bladder infection and are still

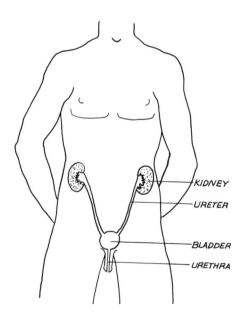

Fig. 27. The Urinary Tract

the most widely prescribed medication, combining effectiveness of action and economy of cost. The broad-spectrum antibiotics such as tetracycline and Declomycin are potent weapons against the usual organisms causing bladder infection, while Furadantin and NegGram are heavy artillery useful in stubborn cases. Pyridium, notable for causing orange-colored urine, is a urinary pain killer; pyridium has no curative value, but its analgesic action helps relieve painful bladder irritation and spasm. In the treatment of bladder infection, the patient should drink large amounts of water, and the use of alcohol should be forbidden. Most bladder infections respond to therapy within two or three days, but treatment should be continued for at least ten days to two weeks to prevent recurrence of the infection.

BLADDER CANCER

"Doctor, I feel fine otherwise, but my urine is blood red." Bladder cancer, not uncommon in senior citizens, usually announces its presence by passage of bloody urine. Burning and frequent urination may be noted, but are usually not present. Symptoms of blood in the urine should be immediately investigated by the doctor, who will usually recommend X rays of the urinary tract and cystoscopy: a look into the bladder through an instrument called the cystoscope.

Carcinoma of the bladder is a slow-growing cancer that spreads to other areas of the bladder wall, but tends to stay within that organ. The tumor usually can be controlled by treatment. In many cases, surgical removal of small bladder tumors through the cystoscope will be performed at regular intervals. X-ray therapy has been used with success in many patients, and instillation of antitumor medication, such as thio-tepa, is sometimes effective in the treatment of multiple small cancer sites within the bladder. The patient with cancer of the bladder can usually look forward to a long life if he is willing to undergo frequent treatment procedures by the urologist.

KIDNEY INFECTION

Infection of the kidney, with pus in the urine associated with back pain and fever, may originate from a bladder infection or begin as bacteria are filtered from the blood. The victim complains of frequent painful urination, shaking chills, fever, and malaise. Examination of the urine will show infection; at times, bloody urine is present.

Infection of the kidney is a serious illness, and aggressive therapy is warranted. Large doses of antibiotics are given orally or by injection. Sulfonamides such as Gantrisin are useful, broad-spectrum antibiotics such as tetracycline or Declomycin are often prescribed, and Loridine may be given by injection in persons unable to take medication by mouth. Severely infected individuals are admitted to the hospital, and intravenous feedings may be required. The patient should receive large quantities of fluid to flush the kidneys. With appropriate therapy, the urinary irritation, fever, and backache are usually relieved within 72 hours, but medication should be continued for at least two weeks to prevent recurrence.

While the first episode of kidney infection will be treated with several weeks of antibiotic therapy, repeated kidney infections call for investigation of the entire urinary tract for a possible cause. In some recurrent cases, long-term use of antibiotics is necessary.

KIDNEY STONES

Kidney stones contain crystals of calcium, phosphate, or uric acid. Uric acid stones are common in gout sufferers, while calcium and phosphate stones may occur in persons drinking large quantities of milk. A stone begins when a microscopic crystal develops in the urine, acting as a focus that snowballs into a tiny but dangerous concretion. Since a scanty intake of fluids predisposes to the formation of all types of urinary crystals, desert nomads are often plagued with kidney stones.

Kidney stones cause no symptoms as long as they remain in the kidney. Pain occurs when the kidney stone begins to migrate, becoming temporarily lodged in the ureter between the kidney and bladder. As the stone becomes trapped in the ureter, the kidney continues to form urine and pushes against the blockage, causing the patient to writhe with severe pain in the involved side. There is tenderness to touch over the kidney area, and telltale blood cells in the urine can be seen through the microscope.

At least half of all kidney stones will exit without assistance if given enough time. The patient should walk around to keep the stone moving, drink glass after glass of water to flush the kidneys, and strain the urine through muslin to net the stone when passed. Antibiotics may be prescribed to prevent infection, and narcotics such as morphine or Demerol are often given as necessary for pain. If the stone has not passed spontaneously after 48 hours, the patient should be seen by a urologist, who may perform cystoscopy and attempt to snare the pebble with an instrument. Attempted removal of stones through the cystoscope is effective about half the time; those shy stones that shun spontaneous passage and refuse to be coaxed out by cystoscopy will require surgery. Chemical analysis of a passed kidney stone can provide important clues to metabolic short circuits and can guide the campaign to prevent future stone formation.

You can help prevent kidney stones:
Take plenty of fluids to keep urinary crystals dissolved.
Avoid consuming too much milk and calcium-containing foods.
Check your blood uric acid level yearly and treat gout promptly.
Correct metabolic abnormalities suggested by stone analysis.

UREMIA

Uremia, the build-up of waste products in the bloodstream caused by kidney failure, is a painless condition and may cause no symptoms other than mild fatigue. Uremia may be the last act in the tragedy of poorly controlled diabetes, severe hypertension, chronic urinary tract infection, or a severe reaction to a medication.

While cases of uremia that represent the final stage of long-standing kidney disease are usually not salvageable, other individuals suffering uremia because of acute illness may survive if wastes can be removed from the blood artificially while the patient recovers from his temporary illness. The artificial kidney is now available at all major medical centers; this complex apparatus, hundreds of times larger than the human kidney, can be lifesaving in selected kidney-failure patients. Physicians on the artificial kidney team must decide whether the benefits of the artificial kidney justify the expense and possible hazards to the patient. In recent years, some patients with incurable kidney disease have been kept alive for long periods, and research is now in progress to make possible the use of artificial kidneys at home in cases of long-standing uremia.

CANCER OF THE KIDNEY

Cancer of the kidney has a moderate degree of malignancy; it is not as highly malignant as cancer of the lung, nor as slow growing as thyroid cancer. Kidney cancer usually manifests itself as blood in the urine, associated with a dull ache in the flank. These symptoms should be promptly reported to the physician, who will order X rays of the kidney and cystoscopy. A renal angiogram, the injection of a dye through the blood vessels to the kidney, may help pinpoint the diagnosis.

Cancer of the kidney is treated by surgical removal of the involved kidney; some patients will be given X-ray therapy following removal of the tumor. The five-year survival rate in this type of cancer is about 35 per cent, and the highest cure rates will be found in those patients who receive prompt diagnosis of the initial warning sign of bloody urine.

Blood Diseases After 65

The tide of blood in me
Hath proudly flow'd in vanity till now.
WILLIAM SHAKESPEARE
(1564-1616)
Henry IV, Part II

THE CHANGES OF AGING

Blood is composed of white and red blood cells suspended in a fluid called serum (see Figure 28). The red blood cells carry oxygen to the tissues and remove carbon dioxide waste products; white blood cells are warriors combating infection. The blood contains other components such as antibodies, plasma cells, blood platelets, and the factors involved in blood clotting.

Normal blood cells are formed in the bone marrow, beginning as infant cells and progressing through a maturing process until the final adult red blood cell is released into the bloodstream. White blood cells arise in the bone marrow, liver, and spleen. Without an adequate intake of protein, vitamins, and iron, the blood cell factories falter.

The problems of aging may influence the composition of the blood. A diet deficient in protein and iron may lead to impaired production of red cells, diminishing the oxygen-carrying capacity of the blood. Fluid retention caused by heart failure may cause a dilution of

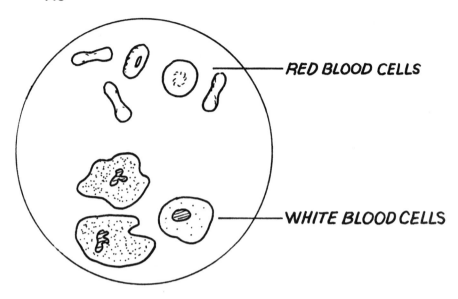

Fig. 28. Blood Cells Seen Through the Microscope

the red blood cells, with the same end result. Impaired intake or absorption of vitamin B_{12} or folic acid may sow the seeds of anemia.

ANEMIA

Anemia is a shortage of able-bodied blood cells. There may be a deficient number of red blood cells, a lack of iron in the cells, or immature red blood cells in the circulation. The symptoms of anemia are weakness, fatigue, and pallor, and in some cases the important clue will be a sore red tongue. The patient lacks his normal energy, and advanced anemia may cause a rapid pulse and shortness of breath.

The most common cause of anemia after age 65 is chronic blood loss subsequent to peptic ulcer or cancer in the stomach or large intestine. The finding of anemia in an older person calls for painstaking investigation with X rays of the entire gastrointestinal tract. Advanced cancer may cause anemia by bleeding into the digestive tract or by spreading to the bone and crowding out the marrow that normally manufactures blood cells. Also common in senior citizens is iron-deficiency anemia, the consequence of diets low in protein and iron.

Proper treatment of anemia demands accurate diagnosis of the cause. Anemia following blood loss from bleeding ulcers or tumors of the intestinal tract should receive prompt therapy of the bleeding site, while anemia caused by replacement of bone marrow by cancer cells needs appropriate anticancer therapy. Iron-deficiency anemia caused by a tea-and-toast diet requires the administration of iron tablets and upgrading the menu to provide adequate amounts of meat and green vegetables.

How to prevent anemia:
Eat meat at least once daily.
Take fruits and vegetables for vitamins.
Avoid "empty-calorie" sweets and starches.
Have the doctor check your hemoglobin at least yearly.

LEUKEMIA AND LYMPHOMA

Leukemia, a term derived from the Greek words meaning "white blood," is an overproduction of white blood cells. While normal white cells in the blood combat infection, leukemia causes the formation of enormous numbers of abnormal white blood cells that provide no defense against bacteria. The legions of abnormal white blood cells crowd the normal blood-producing cells out of the bone marrow and result in a shortage of oxygen-carrying red blood cells and protective white blood cells. Because of the faulty production of blood-clotting factors, easy bruising or nosebleed may be the first hint of leukemia.

The two predominant types of white blood cells are neutrophils (granulocytes) and lymphocytes. In general, neutrophils are active against bacterial infections, and lymphocytes are important against viral infections. In leukemia, either the lymphocytes or the granulocytes will be abnormally increased, and the conditions are called lymphocytic leukemia and granulocytic leukemia. Either type of leukemia may be acute, with a rapid downhill course, or chronic, progressing at a snail's pace over many years.

Hodgkin's disease and lymphosarcoma, together called the lymphomas, are blood diseases not unlike leukemia, characterized by mushrooming lymph glands, with obvious swelling in the neck, underarm area, and groin. There will be enlargement of the liver and spleen, at first detectable only by the physician, but later feeling like a lead weight in the abdomen. With the millions of added cells clamoring for nourishment, there is weight loss and often fever. Replacement of normal bone marrow by abnormal cells brings anemia, with weakness and pallor.

Evidence of leukemia or lymphoma is sometimes present on the blood smear. The bone marrow test—a small amount of bone marrow is removed through a heavy needle from the breastbone or hip—usually clinches the diagnosis of leukemia, while examination of a surgically removed lymph gland is proof positive of lymphoma.

Leukemia and lymphoma are treated with chemical agents and X-ray therapy; the exact choice of therapy depends upon accurate diagnosis under the microscope. Busulfan has been very effective in chronic granulocytic leukemia, while X-ray therapy and nitrogen mustard have been helpful in cases of Hodgkin's disease. Other compounds used in the treatment of leukemia and lymphoma include 6-mercaptopurine, chlorambucil, cyclophosphamide, vincristine, prednisone, and others.

While there have been some cures of very early stages of Hodgkin's disease, there are virtually no cures of leukemia. Leukemia sufferers show a variable life span: the average duration of life in chronic granulocytic leukemia is 3.2 years, and in chronic lymphocytic leukemia, 5.4 years, although many afflicted oldsters live to scoff at these statistics.

MULTIPLE MYELOMA

Multiple myeloma is an overproduction of plasma cells, normally a minor component of the blood. Multiple myeloma must be considered a leukemia of the plasma cells, the symptoms of which are caused by colossal numbers of myeloma cells crowding the marrow of bone. Broken ribs and vertebrae are stark evidence of invading tumor cells. Bone destruction, releasing calcium and phosphorus into the bloodstream, will impair calcium metabolism, and there may be profound anemia and bleeding, as seen in leukemia.

A blood smear may reveal rouleaux, a stacking of the blood cells like poker chips (see Figure 29). The urine often carries a characteristic albumin called Bence-Jones protein, found only in myeloma, but the diagnosis will usually require examination of the bone marrow.

If the disease has been detected early, there should be prompt response to therapy with melphalan or cyclophosphamide. However, many cases are not detected until the late stages; when far advanced, multiple myeloma is a progressive, inevitably fatal disease, and the outlook will depend upon the stage of the disease when first discovered. The life expectancy with multiple myeloma is one to three years,

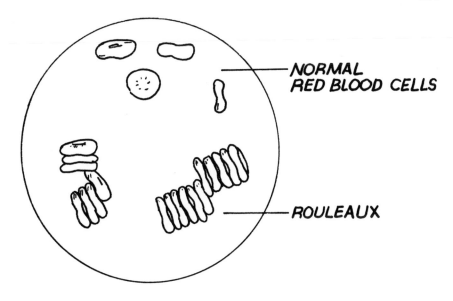

NORMAL
RED BLOOD CELLS

ROULEAUX

Fig. 29. Stacked Red Blood Cells as Seen Through the Microscope

although I have one elderly patient still alive and alert eight years following the discovery of her disease.

PERNICIOUS ANEMIA

Pernicious anemia results from a deficiency of vitamin B_{12}. Patients with the disease are unable to absorb this vitamin through the wall of the stomach in spite of adequate intake by mouth. Vitamin B_{12} is necessary for the newly formed blood cells to reach maturity; in pernicious anemia, red blood cells remain adolescent, and these immature blood cells are released into the bloodstream.

The immature blood cells have a reduced oxygen-carrying capacity and cannot shoulder the load of adult red cells. Victims of pernicious anemia suffer pallor and weakness, as with any other type of anemia, often linked with an impairment of the nerves down the legs causing a loss of balance and an awkward gait.

The physician will diagnose pernicious anemia by examining the blood smear and finding large immature blood cells.

Pernicious anemia is treated by regular replacement of vitamin B_{12} by injection. The minimum injection should be 100 micrograms per month; most indivduals receive a generous 1000 micrograms monthly, with prompt disappearance of all symptoms. Because there is a permanent failure of vitamin B_{12} absorption, the pernicious anemia sufferer must continue monthly injections for the rest of his life.

The Nervous System and the Senior Citizen

It is the mind, and not the limbs, that taints by long sitting.

CHARLES LAMB
(1775-1834)
Letter to Bernard Barton
November 22, 1823

THE CHANGES OF AGING

The brain and spinal cord show a gradual but progressive slowdown after age 65. As hardening of the arteries reduces the blood flow, there is destruction of some nerve cells, which are replaced with nonfunctioning scar tissue. Because hardened arteries to the brain and spinal cord block the extra blood needed for periods of increased activity, the brain fatigues easily, and the capacity for sustained mental effort wanes. The mind balks at memorizing complicated procedures. After a few hours of concentrated reading or writing, eyelids droop and the head begins to nod. Headaches may begin after 65. There may be a gradual loss of coordination, and tremors—shaking of the hands that worsen when one attempts to perform a task—may make their appearance.

153

HEADACHE

"My headaches are driving me crazy!" Headache is one of the most common problems of modern man. While 98 per cent of all headaches in younger persons are caused by nervous tension, after 65 their onset may indicate a more ominous disease. Headaches associated with visual disturbance, weight loss, pain in the eyes, or seizures should be thoroughly investigated.

The tension headache is a dull aching pain across the forehead and temples. This type often occurs when the anxiety is released; the victim notes no symptoms during a long hard work week, only to succumb to a dull throbbing tension headache after dinner or Friday evening. Tension headache usually responds temporarily to aspirin, Tylenol, or Darvon, but the final solution is elimination of the causes of emotional turmoil.

Like tension headache, migraine headache occurs under emotional strain; as with tension headache, its symptoms are caused by an opening of the small blood vessels in the brain, causing a throbbing increased pressure. Migraine is characteristically a severe one-sided headache that lasts from hours to days and is often linked with nausea and spots before the eyes.

Ergotamine preparations such as Cafergot, taken at the first sign of a migraine headache, may prevent it from developing its full severity. Ergotamine prevents the opening of the small blood vessels that causes the headache pain. The agonizing pain of an established migraine headache may be eased by Darvon, Zactirin, or codeine, while severe and frequently recurring migraine headaches may be prevented by daily doses of Sansert or Bellergal.

The hypertensive headache is a dull pounding in the back of the head, worst early in the morning and often coupled with dizziness, although many patients with abnormal elevations of blood pressure suffer no headache. The proper treatment of a hypertensive headache is medication to lower the blood pressure to the normal range.

Other causes of headache include fluid retention, brain tumors, viral illnesses, visual disturbances, and sinus infection. The treatment of the symptomatic headache is accurate diagnosis of the underlying causes and prompt therapy.

TREMORS

Tremor is a shakiness of the hands, common with advancing age, ranging from a mild reaction to anxiety to a severe incapacitating jerking movement that involves the hands and arms. Most tremors are caused by a deficient blood supply to the brain and nerves of the spinal cord. Where nerve cells, deficient in oxygen and vital nutrients, are short-circuited, shakiness begins. Vitamin deficiency or drug reactions can cause shakiness. Tremors early in the morning that are relieved by whiskey, characteristic of the advanced alcoholic, are called "the shakes"—the body's plea for the temperate use of alcohol.

In many cases, mild tremors can be relieved by the daily use of such muscle relaxant-tranquilizer tablets as meprobamate or Valium. More severe tremors may require the use of Artane; Dilantin has been used successfully to control some tremors. Tremors should not be accepted as an inevitable occurrence of old age, but should be presented to the physician for accurate diagnosis and therapy.

PARKINSONISM

Parkinsonism, also called paralysis agitans, is a disease of the nervous system seen almost exclusively after age 65. The victim of Parkinsonism will show a characteristic tremor of the hands as though he were rolling a pill. The face seems to lack expression, there is a ruddy complexion, and the patient walks with small steps holding the arms tightly at the sides. There is difficulty in beginning walking; once in motion, there is trouble stopping. The speech and swallowing mechanisms may be impaired.

The exact cause of Parkinsonism is unknown. Parkinsonism may follow a severe case of flu, and there were thousands of such cases following the flu epidemic of 1918. Parkinsonism appears to be caused by damage to a small discrete area of the brain.

Parkinsonism has been treated with various forms of therapy. Often prescribed is a medication to reduce tremor such as Artane or Akineton. The recent introduction of L-Dopa has dramatically changed the drug therapy of Parkinsonism in patients able to tolerate the drug's significant side effects. Some severely incapacitated individuals have been referred for brain surgery, with selective destruction of a tiny trigger area within the brain; the results have been fair, with a few dramatic recoveries.

At present, there is no known way to prevent Parkinsonism.

SEIZURES

The convulsive seizure victim characteristically loses consciousness and falls to the floor, with an initial twitching of the arms and legs. The eyes roll back, there is a chewing motion of the jaw that often injures the tongue, and there may be loss of control of the bowels and bladder. In an 1840 London lecture, Thomas Carlyle remarked, "A man is not strong who takes convulsion-fits; though six men cannot hold him then."

Seizures are the hallmark of epilepsy, which rarely begins after age 65. Seizures may occur because of uncontrolled hypertension, stroke, meningitis, or high fever; the onset of repeated seizures after 65 may be the first sign of brain tumor.

The initial management of the acute seizure is to prevent harm to the patient. He should be rolled on his side so that, if he vomits, the vomitus will not be inhaled into the lungs. A man's belt or similar firm but pliable material should be placed between the teeth. (Do not place your finger between the teeth!) A feverish patient should be sponged to reduce the temperature. A doctor should be summoned, but the patient should be left on the floor, allowing time for the convulsion to abate. Resist the temptation to do more. Convulsions almost always subside spontaneously, and further attempts at first aid, such as moving the patient or forcing fluids into the mouth, may be dangerous.

The initial therapy of the acute convulsion is followed by exhaustive medical investigation to uncover the cause. A spinal tap will be necessary, and skull X rays and a radioactive brain scan may be done. Once evaluated, most epileptic seizures can be controlled by anticonvulsive medication such as Dilantin or phenobarbital. Blood pressure must be controlled, meningitis or infection will be treated with huge doses of antibiotics, and possible brain tumors are referred to the neurosurgeon for appropriate therapy.

BRAIN TUMORS

Tumors of the brain can occur at any age and are not uncommon in the senior citizen. Brain tumors show great variation in the degree of malignancy, from very slow-growing tumors that may persist for many years to a highly malignant cancer, with life expectancy measured in weeks to months. Meningioma is a fortunately slow-growing tumor that arises in the lining cells of the brain, causing headache and visual symptoms. Although most meningiomas can be safely removed by neurosurgery, the tumor may recur and require repeated surgery.

Other brain tumors are much more troublesome, with the glioblastoma multiforme showing the most rapid progression. Malignant brain tumors cause headache, vomiting, and altered consciousness. Advanced cases will show weight loss, with weakness of one side of the face or one arm and leg similar to a stroke.

Suspected brain tumors require medical investigation with spinal tap, skull X rays, and brain scan. Surgery is the preferred treatment if removal of the tumor seems possible, although X-ray treatment and chemotherapy are used in some cases. The outlook for the brain tumor victim is poor, but the exact prognosis depends upon the type of tumor and the stage when first detected.

Mrs. Senior Citizen

Women and music should never be dated.
OLIVER GOLDSMITH
(1728-1774)
She Stoops to Conquer

AFTER THE MENOPAUSE

Menopause, the cessation of menstrual periods that occurs about age 45 to 50, has been the subject of considerable folklore. At the time of the menopause, the ovaries, which have controlled the monthly menstrual flow, gradually cease to function. The lining cells of the womb no longer grow and recede each month, prepared to receive a fertilized egg and discharging blood when none is received. The periods cease, and the childbearing years draw to a close.

The loss of normal ovarian function after the menopause can cause mischief persisting until after age 65; the most notable of these is the hot flush, the dilation of the tiny blood vessels under the skin, with waves of extreme warmth engulfing the body. Hot flushes are unpredictable, occurring at inconvenient times and perhaps awakening the sufferer at night. A direct result of ovarian deficiency, they are caused by high blood levels of a pituitary hormone that normally guides the ebb and flow of ovarian hormones. Although irritability and anxiety are commonly accepted trademarks of the menopause, most of the emotional ups and downs of the menopausal years can be attributed to such other factors in the patient's life as rebellious teenagers, children leaving for college, financial insecurity, or fantasies of departing beauty. Nervousness and irritability tend to rise as ovarian hormones fall, just as the week before the menstrual period in a younger woman—when hormones are at their lowest—may be clouded by overwhelming irritability. Fatigue and headaches, common after the menopause, may reflect anxiety-producing forces in the patient's life or may in reality be the result of waning ovarian function.

It should be emphasized that the menopausal symptoms are annoying, but mild in severity. The years following menopause, with lessened family responsibilities and relief from the threat of possible pregnancy, should be a time of increased fulfillment for Mrs. Senior Citizen.

HOW ABOUT HORMONES?

Many of the physical symptoms of the menopause follow a drop in estrogenic hormones. Estrogen, produced by the normal ovary, helps keep the skin young, sustains vaginal tissues, maintains breast fullness, and preserves firm bones. Estrogens enhance the formation of normal blood cells, help to maintain normal growth of hair, and impart the vitality seen in the younger woman.

Following the menopause, women suffer increased hardening of the arteries and a higher incidence of heart attacks and hypertension. There may be a softening of the bones, leading to a reduction in height and "dowager's hump." Older women may experience thinning of the hair, wrinkling of the skin, and a painful irritation of the vaginal tissues, all related to a shortage of estrogenic hormones after the menopause.

Over the past decade, the administration of hormone tablets following the menopause has gained increased favor with physicians. The menopausal woman showing symptoms of hot flushes, backache, vaginal irritation, and fatigue is examined thoroughly, and a Pap test is checked for cancer. The physician may prescribe estrogens such as Premarin or Menest, to be taken regularly except during a rest period of 5 to 7 days a month. Almost all women beginning hormone therapy report prompt cessation of menopausal symptoms, with waxing vitality and waning hot flushes.

Hormone therapy has its problems. Dosage must be carefully regulated to prevent vaginal bleeding, there may be breast tenderness, and some women develop worrisome breast cysts, not to mention an apparent increased incidence of phlebitis of the legs.

All in all, women receiving postmenopausal estrogen therapy look younger and feel vigorous longer than their sisters who remain hormone-poor. Your family doctor can advise whether the benefits of hormone therapy outweigh its possible hazards for you.

THE LUMP IN THE BREAST

Discovering a lump in the breast is a terrifying experience for a woman of any age. The lump may feel like a pea or marble under the skin. Usually firm and movable between the fingers, most solid growths are painless, and the presence of pain or tenderness suggests that the lump is likely to be a harmless cyst. A lump under the arm should be considered as serious as a lump in the breast, and all suspected growths in either area should be presented to the physician for accurate diagnosis.

The doctor will examine both breasts and both underarm areas. He may order breast X rays called mammograms; in my experience, however, mammograms are not 100 per cent reliable as a means of detecting the presence of cancer, and the final diagnosis of the lump in the breast should be left to the surgeon.

Most lumps should be removed for accurate diagnosis. Because early breast cancer is curable by total removal of the growth, delay to "see what happens in a month" is like playing Russian roulette—the stakes are too high. In a few cases, fluid-filled cysts may be drained with a needle and the fluid sent to the laboratory for analysis. At least one of every ten breast lumps will be malignant; the surgical removal of the questionable lump results in a one-inch-long barely noticeable breast scar in the other nine cases. Prompt removal of malignancy affords the best possible chance of cure for cancer.

If a biopsy shows breast cancer, the entire breast and underarm lymph glands are removed in an operation called a radical mastectomy. Following surgery, X-ray therapy may be recommended to pick up cancer cells that may have escaped. Once the surgical site is healed, the patient will be fitted with special undergarments so that, with proper choice of clothes, the absence of the breast is not noticeable.

Breast cancer shows a disturbing tendency to lie dormant following radical mastectomy and then to recur after a lapse of three to five years as a lump in the other breast or a sudden fracture, indicating the spread of cancer to the bone. Tumors that have journeyed beyond the breast are treated with X-ray therapy or hormones, depending upon the age of the patient and the stage of cancer. The overall survival rate in breast cancer in about 60 per cent.

How to check your breasts for lumps:

Lie down on your back with one arm over your head. With the other hand, gently examine all parts of the breast, including the nipple and underarm area. Take your time. Repeat this careful breast examination each month.

VAGINAL INFECTIONS

After 65, the cells of the vagina lack nourishing hormones and are more susceptible to infection that causes pain, itching, and a watery or thick discharge. Vaginal irritation may be caused solely by estrogen shortage, with a local inflammation that will respond to estrogen vaginal cream or tablets; on the other hand, it may be caused by bacteria, a fungus, or a tiny organism called trichomonas. Mixed infections containing all three organisms are not uncommon.

The itching, burning vagina should be presented to the family physician for accurate diagnosis. Monilial infections will present a beefy red shiny appearance, plus a thick cheesy discharge; trichomonas will show a frothy clear vaginal discharge with intense itching; and a bacterial infection will cause a thicker vaginal discharge with pus. A culture may be taken to confirm the diagnosis.

The patient should begin local therapy with hot baths and douching as indicated. A vaginal cream or suppository will be prescribed according to the type of infection. Bacterial infections will often be treated with a sulfa-containing vaginal cream such as Sultrin; monilial vaginal infections usually receive Mycostatin vaginal tablets or Sporastacin vaginal cream; and trichomonas vaginal infections are frequently treated with Flagyl tablets and vaginal suppositories, with the husband also required to take Flagyl tablets. In cases where an estrogen deficiency sets the stage for a vaginal infection, the treatment may include estrogen tablets. All vaginal infections are curable with appropriate therapy, and the sufferer should not long endure her symptoms before reporting for diagnosis and treatment.

DO YOU LOSE YOUR URINE WHEN YOU COUGH?

"Do you lose your urine when you cough?" may sound like an impertinent question; however, if the answer is yes, your troubles probably began many years ago with a difficult childbirth. Large babies, explosive deliveries with torn tissues, and the energetic use of high forceps damage the supporting walls of the vagina. The weakness of vaginal tissues causes few symptoms in the younger woman but, with advancing age, estrogen deficiency and gradual weakening of tissues allow the walls of the vagina to sag (see Figure 30A & B). The front wall of the vagina supports the bladder; when this is weakened, the bladder bulges into the vagina. Examination by the doctor will reveal sagging of the vaginal tissues, and bearing down by the patient will cause bulging through the vaginal opening. There may be an associated weakness of the urethra, which controls urinary flow from the bladder; the condition is called cystocele or urethrocele.

The treatment for cystocele or urethrocele is surgical repair of the weak bladder support; attempts at control with a pessary are advised only for elderly individuals whose health prohibits all elective surgery. Following the operation, most patients report good control of urination.

PROLAPSE OF THE UTERUS

In prolapse of the uterus (see Figure 30C), the womb protrudes through the vaginal opening when one stands. Prolapse of the uterus is caused by weakened tissues after the menopause and is linked to the twin

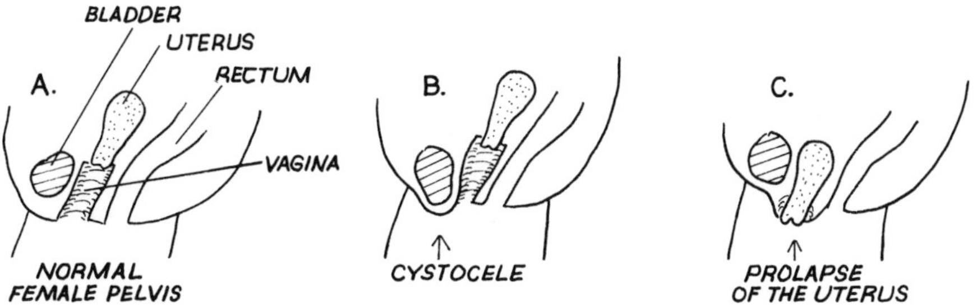

Fig. 30. Pelvic Support Problems

perils of previous childbirth tears and waning hormone levels. Since the protruding mouth of the womb is easy prey for irritation, infection, and bleeding, elderly women with this condition will often wear a sanitary napkin to protect the mouth of the womb from trauma. A surprising number of elderly ladies erroneously consider prolapse of the uterus a normal condition of aging.

The treatment of prolapse of the uterus is surgery. Attempted control with a pessary, requiring frequent pelvic examinations to remove and clean the device, is only for those women in whom old age and disease prevent operative repair. The surgeon may remove the uterus, a hysterectomy, or may close the vagina with the womb sewn up inside, eliminating further protrusion.

FIBROID TUMORS

Fibroid tumors are benign growths occurring on the uterus, common from ages 30 to 90 (see Figure 31). There is no spread to distant areas, and they are not cancerous. The fibroid tumors are knots of muscle cells of the womb that may grow as large as a grapefruit. In fact, some neglected fibroids have become large enough to mimic pregnancy. Fibroid tumors may cause troublesome recurrent bleeding.

The only treatment of fibroid tumors is surgical removal. In younger women, the fibroid tumor may be carefully removed from the wall of the uterus, leaving the womb intact for further childbearing. When fibroid tumors are removed after age 65, usually because of pain or bleeding, a hysterectomy should be performed to remove both the uterus and the tumor. Small symptomfree fibroid tumors may be safely followed, with examination at six-month intervals to detect possible change in size.

CANCER OF THE UTERUS

Cancer of the uterus, not uncommon in older women, begins with vaginal bleeding, perhaps accompanied by a vaginal discharge of brown or yellow material. The doctor will suspect cancer of the uterus after performing a physical examination with a Pap test. A tiny piece of tissue taken by instrument from inside the womb will be examined in the laboratory to confirm the presence or absence of uterine cancer.

Cancer of the uterus is treated with surgery or radiation. Surgical removal of the uterus and both ovaries may allow cure; radiation is used

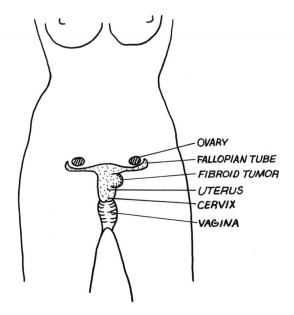

OVARY
FALLOPIAN TUBE
FIBROID TUMOR
UTERUS
CERVIX
VAGINA

Fig. 31. Fibroid Tumor of the Uterus

in many cases, either postoperatively or in cases not amenable to surgery. Cancer of the cervix, the mouth of the womb, is more common in middle-aged women than in those after 65; radiation is the usual therapy.

CANCER OF THE OVARY

Cancer of the ovary carries a high mortality because the growth remains in hiding, causing no symptoms until the malignancy is far advanced. Early evidence of cancer of the ovary is a nagging pain in one lower side of the abdomen plus a sensation of abdominal fullness, which usually indicates a well-developed tumor. Advanced disease will cause weight loss, pallor, and loss of appetite.

The treatment of cancer of the ovary is surgical removal of the tumor, with the highest cure rate found in those cancers detected early, usually on routine examination before symptoms begin. Since many ovarian cancers begin as ovarian cysts, the surgical removal of the cyst removes the threat of cancer. X-ray therapy and chemotherapy have been used in some resistant cases. All complaints of persistent abdominal pain should be evaluated by the family doctor to allow the earliest possible detection and treatment of ovarian cancer.

Mr.
Senior
Citizen

STRICTURE

Stricture of the urethra, a common cause of urinary blockage in men after 65, is a scar in the tube leading from the bladder out through the penis. The stricture blocks the urinary stream, with retention of urine in the bladder; the back pressure of the urine may reach as far as the kidneys, causing slow but progressive kidney damage.

The stricture of the urethra forms painlessly and gradually, usually as scar tissue following some inflammation occurring many years ago. A case of gonorrhea or injury to the penis as a young adult may lead to urethral stricture after age 65.

Urethral stricture is treated by surgical correction whenever possible, but many strictures lie in areas that thwart surgery, and these are treated with repeated dilations, stretching the tube to enlarge the opening. Dilations keep the flow of urine free and must be repeated at regular intervals throughout the life of the stricture victim.

THE LUMP IN THE SCROTUM

The discovery of a lump (see Figure 32) in the scrotum in a male may be compared to finding a lump in the breast in the female. The scrotal lump, usually found by accident, may be tender, is usually firm, and almost always moves freely beneath the skin.

The scrotal lump may be a spermatocele—a collection of sperm in a partially blocked tube from the testicle. Usually firm and painless, a spermatocele feels like a large marble in the scrotum. The spermatocele is harmless, and if the doctor is sure of the diagnosis, removal is not necessary.

An enlarged hernia, descending into the scrotum, will cause a scrotal lump extending into the inguinal area. The hernia will transmit pressure from the abdomen upon coughing.

A hydrocele is a fluid-filled sac around the testicle, and an ordinary flashlight placed against the hydrocele in a partially darkened room will show the obvious presence of fluid. Except for very small ones, hydroceles should be removed surgically to prevent enlargement in later years. Some hydroceles are treated by needle removal of the fluid at regular intervals, when surgery is out of the question because of illness or debility.

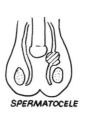

SPERMATOCELE

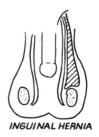

INGUINAL HERNIA

HYDROCELE

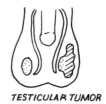

TESTICULAR TUMOR

Fig. 32. The Lump in the Scrotum

The lump in the scrotum may be cancer of the testicle. Textbooks describe cancer of the testicle as a disease of younger men, but some cases occur after 65, and all suspected tumors should be surgically explored. If malignant, the involved testicle will be removed, and the operation will be followed by removal of local lymph glands and possible radiation therapy. Carcinoma of the testicle has a moderate to high degree of malignancy, and prompt removal of all tumors is essential.

EPIDIDYMITIS

The epididymis is a narrow tube carrying the sperm from the testicle up the inguinal canal through the abdominal cavity and into the storage sacs at the base of the penis. Epididymitis is an infection of this tube, which lies largely in the scrotum, causing fever, pain, and swelling of the scrotum on the involved side. Sometimes there is an associated infection in the urine or prostate.

Epididymitis is treated with large doses of antibiotics and cold packs to shrink scrotal swelling. A support called a scrotal sling is worn to relieve pressure, and Darvon or codeine is given as necessary for pain. The infection will usually subside within two to four days after antibiotics are begun.

HERNIA

A hernia is a weakness of the muscular wall of the abdomen through which the intestine protrudes to form a lump under the skin. A hernia may occur through the navel or through an old surgical incision, but most hernias are found in the groin. The groin hernia is called the inguinal hernia because it lies next to the inguinal ligament; if sufficiently large, the inguinal hernia may extend into the scrotum (see Figure 32).

Inguinal hernias are an ever-present danger because the intestine may become snared in the opening, requiring surgery to prevent gangrene. Because of the possibility of such entrapment and because hernias often enlarge with advancing age, all such defects should be repaired surgically soon after their discovery. The operation is a simple one, requiring only a week in the hospital, and the benefit to the patient far outweighs the hazards. The use of a hernia truss should be allowed only in those patients too ill or infirm to be good surgical risks.

ENLARGED PROSTATE

The prostate gland surrounding the urethra just below the bladder (see Figure 33) is influenced by the production of male hormones. The prostate is small during adolescent years and begins during the 20's and 30's to enlarge in response to male hormones; by age 65 or 70 the ballooning gland may squeeze off the flow of urine through the urethra. Prostatic enlargement occurs in such an irregular fashion that the blockage of urine is dependent, not so much upon the size of the prostate, as upon the enlargement of the lobe adjacent to the urethra.

The obstructing prostate requires surgical correction once the patient notes such symptoms as difficulty initiating the urinary stream and hesitancy of urination—passing urine in a stuttering fashion. The stream may be narrow and the sufferer may arise from bed to pass urine three or four times each night.

The prostate may be removed through an abdominal operation or snipped away with an instrument introduced through the penis. The choice of the operation is determined by the size of the prostate gland and the surgeon's judgment. Although there may be a brief period of urinary leakage following the operation, the long-term results of prostatic surgery are usually quite good, and the operation is recommended for all mature males with troublesome prostatic enlargement.

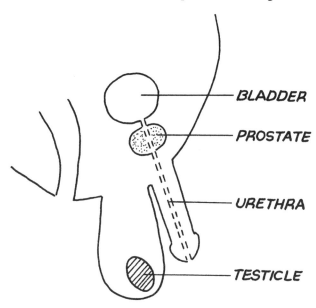

Fig. 33. The Prostate Gland

PROSTATE INFECTION

Infection in the prostate is a common disease of adult males, found in men from ages 20 to 90. Prostatic infection begins with congestion in the prostate, often following a long trip in a vehicle, such as the family car; prostatitis is therefore an occupational disease of traveling salesmen, delivery men, and truck drivers. Alcohol will aggravate the inflammation. The victim of prostatitis will show a frequent need to urinate, burning upon urination, and a dull pain at the base of the penis. Because the infection in the prostate does not drain readily, the inflammation remains trapped in the gland and may become a chronic problem.

Prostatic infection is treated with antibiotics, such as sulfonamides, tetracyclines, or Declomycin. Furadantin has been helpful, particularly in cases accompanied by bladder infection. Long automobile trips and alcohol are forbidden. A hot tub bath once or twice a day often brings relief. Prostatic massage, the application of pressure to the prostate gland through the rectum by the doctor, helps to squeeze secretions from the prostate gland, affording relief to some sufferers. Infection of the prostate shows a distressing tendency to return, and prostatitis sufferers may experience flare-ups of their disease from time to time.

How to prevent prostatitis:
Avoid prolonged sitting and long trips in the car.
Do not take alcohol.
Have regular sexual relations.
Drink plenty of water.
Treat all urinary infections promptly.

CANCER OF THE PROSTATE

Prostatic cancer is a slow-growing tumor, with recorded cases of individuals surviving 20 to 25 years after detection of the disease. The early cancer of the prostate has no symptoms, but the tumor may be detected during a routine checkup in the doctor's office. Advanced tumors cause symptoms of prostatic enlargement, with difficulty in initiating and sustaining the urinary stream.

Cancer of the prostate, like the prostate gland itself, is dependent upon male hormones; therefore the treatment of prostatic cancer is directed at reversing the hormonal pattern of the body. The testicles are often removed, eliminating the fountain of male hormones; the patient begins regular doses of female hormones, either as oral medication, such as TACE, or monthly injections of a long-acting compound called Estradurin. Males undergoing this treatment program will sometimes see enlargement of the breasts and collect fat around the hips, but this is a small price to pay for the many years of life afforded by the hormonal method of cancer treatment. Along with the hormonal therapy, the prostate gland will be removed surgically if symptoms of urinary obstruction occur. The early detection of the small prostate nodule is testimony to the importance of the annual physical examination.

Sex and the Senior Citizen

That which distinguishes man from the beast is drinking without being thirsty and making love at all seasons.

PIERRE DE BEAUMARCHAIS
(1732-1799)

THE MATURE MARRIAGE

Yes, Virginia, there is sex after 65. Even after 40 years of living together, marriage should continue to bloom. Husband and wife have passed through young adulthood and middle age together and now are entering the retirement years, the period of fulfillment when marriage can grow to maturity,

Marriage is more than eating and sleeping together; it's a sharing of adventures and memories. It's knowing when your wife would like breakfast in bed and sensing when your husband wants to leave the party. The mature marriage is a lifetime of experiences and a future of plans.

What about sex and the senior citizen? Sigmund Freud, the father of psychoanalysis, originally conceived of sex as the pleasurable stimulation of the body; the sexual relationship between husband and wife includes holding hands in a restaurant, brushing the speck of lint off his lapel, helping her on with her coat, and the goodnight kiss. Sexuality is a reflection of self-esteem. "It is the prime duty of a woman of this terrestrial world to look well," wrote Sir William Osler in 1913, and his advice holds true for the older woman in particular. The couple who trouble to dress for dinner and make themselves attractive will probably be those most vigorous sexually. The unkempt person reflects his lack of self-esteem and seems to proclaim to the world that he is sexually incapable. Does this concept hold true for young people today? It is something to reflect on.

A SECOND HONEYMOON

Many women, whose sexual enjoyment had been clouded by the fear of unplanned pregnancy, have reached their full sexual fulfillment in their 50's, 60's and 70's. There is no reason why the mature woman cannot enjoy normal sexual relations until the late 70's. Regular sexual relations are important in maintaining the integrity of the vaginal tissues; a prolonged period of sexual abstinence, such as a year or two, will result in the formation of scar tissue around the walls of the vagina, and subsequent sexual relations may cause discomfort. Most men retain sexual potency into their 70's. Sexual potency is a measure of the man's confidence and self-esteem; the sexually active senior citizen will be the robust man who is vigorously engaged in hobbies, golf, and community activities.

The retirement years should be an idyllic period. Monthly menstrual flow is no longer a problem, there are no young children to pop in at inconvenient times, and even the telephone doesn't ring as often as it used to. This is the time for the mature couple to enjoy the sexuality of their marriage despite anachronistic Victorian concepts that sexual activity should gradually cease after the menopausal years. With the improved health of our senior citizens, the extra years that have been added to the life span, and the control of many of the diseases of aging, there is no reason why the mature healthy couple should not continue a vigorous sex life.

PAINFUL INTERCOURSE

Painful intercourse is called dyspareunia and refers to pain in the vagina during the sex act. Vaginal inflammation may be caused by deficient estrogen content in the vaginal cells, which is treatable with estrogen vaginal cream and perhaps estrogen pills by mouth. The response to estrogen replacement therapy is dramatic; symptoms of painful intercourse should be relieved within several weeks.

Painful sexual relations may be the result of infection in the vagina, commonly caused by bacteria, yeast, or trichomonas. Treatment of the specific infection will brighten the marital bedroom.

Painful sexual relations may result when a widow remarries and is dismayed to find that the vaginal tissues have shrunken and that attempted sexual relations cause pain, often with tearing of the vaginal lining and bleeding. Postmenopausal shrinkage of the vaginal cells demands estrogen therapy, both in tablet form and the application of an estrogen vaginal cream. The vaginal lining must be stretched, at first by the doctor in his office; later the patient will be shown how to stretch the tissues at home with her fingers. Eventually, careful sexual relations with adequate lubrication will be allowed.

Finally, dyspareunia can be initiated by emotional tension, causing painful tightening of the muscles around the vagina. The treatment is to learn to relax both the muscles and the emotions.

Because adequate sexual relations help to sustain the mature marriage, it is important that all cases of painful sexual relations be brought to the attention of the doctor for diagnosis and treatment. With time and appropriate medication, most causes of painful sexual relations are curable.

IMPOTENCE

The failure of the male partner to sustain an erection is a common cause of sexual problems after age 65. While extreme old age may cause loss of sexual potency along with debility in other areas, the impotent but otherwise healthy man in his 60's should not blame his problem on the changes of aging. An isolated case of diabetes or abnormality of the nervous system may bring a loss of sexual potency, but the vast majority of instances of occasional or chronic loss of sexual potency may be attributed to psychological causes.

Drooping sexual potency reflects a feeling of unworthiness. The sexually inadequate male is the man who has spent all day sitting transfixed in front of the television set, or perhaps the man who has been nagged by the family since awakening in the morning, or the man whose wife frequently reminds him of his failures at work, at home, and in bed.

Since the causes of sexual impotency are usually psychological, the treatment must be psychotherapeutic. The patient must understand the emotional nature of his problem. A complete physical examination must be done, reassuring the patient that no physical cause is present.

The problem should be discussed both with the husband and wife, enlisting the wife's cooperation and patience. On occasion, tablets containing male hormones or thyroid hormone have been prescribed, but their value in this condition is questionable. When I was an intern, I was told of a urologist who treated his elderly impotent patients with a compound called methylene blue, which turns the urine bright azure; he assured his patients that, when the urine turned blue, their "nature" would return. In many cases it worked, showing the psychological nature of the disease. Profound impotence, often coupled with depression, may require psychotherapy to unearth the cause of the psychological disability.

FRIGIDITY

Frigidity is the failure of the female partner to reach a climax during the sex act. Except in cases of dyspareunia, frigidity has the same psychological origin as impotence in the male, reflecting a feeling of unworthiness. Because women are emotionally more complicated than men, however, other factors influence frigidity.

The female who fails to achieve orgasm during the sex act should have a frank discussion with her doctor following a thorough examination. The discussion should include the husband, whose cooperation should be solicited. The doctor may suggest that the husband woo his wife, perhaps with flowers and wine. When making love, he should slow down, making allowance for the wife's slower sexual responses. The doctor will explain that the clitoris, a knot of tissue at the front of the vaginal opening, is the most sexually responsive part of the female organs, and that the husband's stimulation of the clitoris, either manually or by moving forward during the sex act, may help arouse the female sexually and help overcome frigidity.

Cases of long-standing frigidity often have their roots in childhood attitudes. In the sexually liberated 1970's, it is hard to remember the repressive attitudes prevalent when our senior citizens first learned that babies weren't delivered by the stork. Women who were reared in the beliefs that sex is dirty and that "nice girls don't enjoy sex" often find it difficult to enjoy the mature marriage.

With vigorous good health, plus a modern understanding of sexuality and its relationship to marriage, the mature couple should enjoy a mutually satisfying sexual relationship.

Home Care
of the
Senior Citizen

Stay, stay at home, my heart, and rest;
Home-keeping hearts are happiest,
For those that wander they know not where
are full of trouble and full of care;
To stay at home is best.
HENRY WADSWORTH LONGFELLOW
(1807-1882)

WHERE IS THE BEST CARE AVAILABLE?

When her 76-year-old father became too old to change the screens, vacuum the carpet, and keep the kitchen tidy, Mrs. Jones brought him home to live with her family. Shortly after his arrival, however, problems began to emerge. Elderly eyesight caused frequent minor accidents, with broken dishes and ashtrays; to avoid tumbles on the stairs to the second floor, her father took his nap on the living room sofa. Mrs. Jones began having cross words with her husband, who complained that they no longer had privacy, and her son seemed to be pouting constantly, since he had been forced to vacate his room for his grandfather. He and his brother, forced to share a room, fought constantly.

Then disaster struck. Mrs. Jones' father caught the flu from one of the teenage grandsons, and Mrs. Jones found that she was performing nursing duties day and night. With his high fever, her father could not leave his bed to go to the bathroom, and a bedpan was purchased. In spite of constant care, Mrs. Jones seemed unable to keep the bedclothes changed and her patient clean. He seemed to need fresh pajamas constantly. Vomiting began, and Mrs. Jones did not realize that aspirin could be given rectally. Finally, just as the patient seemed to be improving, he arose from the bed one night, slipped on a scatter rug, and shattered his right hip.

COULD THIS TRAGEDY HAVE BEEN PREVENTED?

Down the street lived Mrs. Brown, who also had a 76-year-old father. When his vision and vitality declined, Mr. and Mrs. Brown discussed the problem and decided, "If we plan properly, we should be able to give father the proper care." The old playroom on the main floor, with an adjoining bathroom, was converted into a bedroom. In anticipation of the patient's impaired strength and coordination, firm handrails were installed on the walls near the tub and toilet, and a nightlight glowed constantly near the bathroom door. Scatter rugs were discarded and the thick film of slippery wax was removed from the hardwood floor. Mr. and Mrs. Brown surveyed the results: "Now we're ready for father."

Shortly after the arrival, the Brown's family physician examined the patient, and arrangements were made for regular home health care by the visiting nurse. The Brown's minister stopped by to bid welcome to the community and promised to make regular calls. The patient's library and coin collection were moved into his small bedroom, and a portable television set came as an early Christmas gift. With a room to call his own, Mrs. Brown's father seemed quite content.

When Mrs. Brown's father developed the weakness and fever of flu, the doctor was summoned, and he prescribed daily home nursing visits. Mrs. Brown borrowed a hospital bed with side rails from the county loan service; the public health nurse showed Mrs. Brown how to bathe a patient in bed and how to make a bed with the patient lying in it. The proper use of a bedpan and urinal was explained. With medication and good nursing care by Mrs. Brown, the patient made a prompt recovery and was allowed to sit in an easy chair at the bedside on the fifth day after his illness began. A happy ending.

Across the street lived Mrs. Smith, who also had a 76-year-old father in failing health. Mr. and Mrs. Smith discussed the problem, "Let's realize that our house lacks a spare bedroom and, by past experience, we know that the children can't share a bedroom for more than ten minutes without mayhem." The Smith's single second floor bathroom was already overcrowded; since the Smith children had entered school, Mrs. Smith had resumed teaching second grade and was out of the home six hours each day.

After careful consideration, Mr. and Mrs. Smith decided that they should investigate rest homes in the area. Four miles north of town was a rest home, highly recommended by their local doctor. The Smiths visited the rest home and talked to the administrator, who described how the home had begun as a boarding house and how, with increased demand, two large wings had been added, providing many new private and semiprivate rooms with baths. The rooms were all on one floor. The patients ate in a large, brightly painted and airy dining room, and the diet was tailored to the appetites of elderly persons. A solarium with a television furnished recreation.

Mr. and Mrs. Smith were pleased to learn that her father's Social Security check and his small pension would just about cover the monthly payments for room and board at the rest home.

Mrs. Smith's father chose a semiprivate room, which he promptly decorated with mementoes of an active lifetime. In came his portable television set and favorite rocking chair. Her father was pleased to find friends his own age with a passion for bridge and shuffleboard. On weekend outings at the Smith residence, he spoke glowingly of the new life that he had found in his own room at the rest home.

CONFRONT YOUR FEELINGS

Mrs. Jones, Mrs. Brown, and Mrs. Smith faced the same problem of an elderly parent unable to live alone. Each handled the problem in her own way. In two cases the results were gratifying, and the senior citizen was able to achieve a degree of independence. In Mrs. Jones' case, however, difficulties made their debut on the first day and continued as long as her father was in the home, eventually ending in tragedy. Mrs. Jones' problems arose from a lack of preparation and an ill-advised decision to take her father into the home, which lacked the facilities to care for a disabled elderly person. A few hours spent studying simple techniques of home-nursing care could have prevented grief, but Mrs. Jones did not acquaint herself with the home health aids available. If Mrs. Jones had examined her home for possible causes of calamity, treacherous scatter rugs would have been removed.

If she was so ill-equipped and ill-prepared, why did Mrs. Jones bring her father home? Money is probably not the answer. Most senior citizens have pensions or Social Security checks that will almost cover the cost of their care in a modest rest home. Companionship is certainly not the reason, because any rest home will give the older person infinitely more companionship than living in a home with younger family members who are wrapped up in their own lives.

Most ill-advised decisions to take a disabled elderly relative into the home arise from the senior citizen's fantasies of rejection and the children's pangs of guilt. Persons in their late 60's and 70's should strive for independence. Each individual should have a place of his own, but the senior citizen's children should not need to prove their love by making room in an already crowded home.

Psychologists tell us that guilt feelings are the basis of many neuroses. The act of permitting a parent to achieve independence in a boarding house or retirement village can cause severe guilt feelings in the children, prompting the child to insist that the parent give up a wholesome life with his retirement contemporaries and move in with the younger family. Such misplaced guilt feelings can lead to unhappiness for both the parent and child. Mrs. Brown and Mrs. Smith confronted their guilt feelings and dealt with them realistically, making the correct decisions for their fathers. Mrs. Jones, in her imprudent attempt at home care for her father, reacted to her guilt feeling to the detriment of both her father and her family.

CONSIDER THE NEW FAMILY STRUCTURE

When an elderly disabled person moves into the home, the family structure changes. Some aspects of the new family framework will be as obvious as another place at the dinner table, while others will be subtle and may become apparent only after some time has elapsed. The problems discussed in this chapter should be considered before a decision is made to bring a senior family member into the household.

The young housewife is the absolute monarch of her kitchen; will she tolerate an elderly mother-in-law helping with the preparation of meals, or will she welcome the extra pair of hands? Will the husband hit the ceiling if grandpa uses his workshop tools, or will he welcome seasoned help in keeping up the home repairs? Will there be a power struggle as the elderly citizen exerts his rank, or will grandfather defer to the opinions of more vigorous, younger family members? Will the grandparent welcome service as a babysitter for youngsters in the family, or will the children's shouts at play set his teeth on edge? Will teenagers be proud to bring friends home to meet their grandfather or will the grandparent be peevish and critical? As Logan Pearsall Smith wrote, "The denunciation of the young is a necessary part of the hygiene of older people, and greatly assists the circulation of their blood." Will trips be forsaken to stay home with an elderly family member, will grandfather be a reliable caretaker at vacation time, or might grandfather be fun to have along on vacation?

Will the senior citizen fall in step with the pace of life in the household, or will he have two left feet in family activities? If your honest instincts tell you that having your mother-in-law or father in the home will bring you joy and lighten your burdens, then full speed ahead. However, if a nagging voice tells you that the senior citizen would disrupt the household, then it's in the best interests of the entire family to consider a rest home, retirement village, or boarding house as a permanent residence.

DO YOU HAVE THE FACILITIES?

The facilities necessary for caring for the disabled elderly person will vary from one instance to the next. Ideally, the older person should have his own room at ground level, with adjoining bathroom facilities. Safety rails should be installed near the bathtub and toilet; slippery tub bottoms should have nonskid strips attached. Scatter rugs and slippery floors should be eliminated, as should obstructing furniture and top-heavy lamps.

If the senior citizen has an illness that will require nursing care, a hospital bed, possibly with side rails, can be obtained. Bedpans, urinals, and an emesis basin should be available if needed, and there should be a bell or perhaps a telephone at the bedside to summon help in an emergency. Finally, there must be a devoted daughter or son with the time and interest to carry out the daily nursing chores necessary to maintain the well-being of the elderly family member.

Care
of the
Disabled Patient

*I hope that Lord Grey and you are well—no
easy thing seeing that there are above 1500
diseases to which man is subjected.*

SYDNEY SMITH

(1771-1845)

**Letter to Lady Grey
February 1, 1836**

The next two chapters concern home care of the disabled elderly
patient, with specific topics relevant to a wide variety of disabling
conditions, including stroke, arthritis, chronic brain disease, and acute
illness.

DIET

The senior citizen's stomach functions best when presented with bland
foods, free of the spices and seasoning so palatable to younger appetites. Most elderly persons will find meats and vegetables more to their
liking if they have been boiled or broiled. A blender may be used to
puree meats, vegetables, and fruits, especially if failing strength and
departing dentition make chewing difficult. Modest portions of bland,
appetizing food are required. In my practice, I have found the following
diet useful for most older persons.

GERIATRIC DIET

Bread and Cereals:	White bread, saltines, soda crackers, cooked cereals, rice or corn cereals without nuts or fruit
Fruits:	Fruit juices diluted with water, ripe banana, applesauce, canned peaches or pears, fresh grapefruit
Soups:	Clear, fat-free broth, creamed soup with pureed vegetables
Vegetables:	Pureed or boiled carrots, peas, spinach, asparagus, squash, beets, or lima beans
Potatoes:	Baked, creamed, scalloped, or whipped white potatoes
Meat Products:	Baked, broiled, or roasted beef, lamb, veal, chicken, or turkey
	Broiled, baked, or creamed flounder, sole, tuna, salmon, or haddock
	Liver
Eggs:	Omelet, poached, soft-cooked, or scrambled eggs
Cheese:	Cottage cheese, cream cheese, and American cheese
Desserts:	Pound cake, sponge cake, bread pudding, rice pudding, tapioca pudding, custard
Beverages:	Whole milk, skimmed milk, buttermilk, tea, decaffeinated coffee
Miscellaneous:	Margarine, vegetable oil, macaroni, noodles, spaghetti, rice

Variations in this basic bland soft diet will be made according to the appetite of the patient and the recommendation of the family doctor.

TURNING IN BED

A bedfast patient should be turned from one side to back to other side every few hours to prevent a bedsore, an indolent ulcer over a bony pressure point. Bedsores resist cure, and their prevention is an important goal of good home nursing care.

Since frequent turning of the patient is the key to bedsore prevention, the home attendant must be familiar with the easy method of turning a bedfast invalid. A ballet dancer can easily turn a corpulent fullback if the proper method is used.

The secret to easy turning of the bedfast patient is to move the extremities first, because much of the weight of the body is concentrated in the arms, legs, hips, and shoulders (see Figure 34). When attempting to turn a patient from side to side, you should stand on the side of the bed that you wish the patient to face upon completion of the maneuver. First grasp the hand firmly and bring it as far toward you as possible. Next bend the patient's knee and bring the leg as far across the bed as possible. Then grasp the shoulder and hip of the extremities that have already been positioned and pull these toward you slowly. If you have properly positioned the arm and leg, the body will turn smoothly following the change in weight on the shoulder and hip. To reverse the process and turn the patient to the other side, return your patient to the face-up position, walk around to the other side of the bed, and begin by properly positioning the other arm and leg.

Technique, not force, turns patients. Since the position assumed by the attendant in moving a patient in bed requires bending at the waist, an unnecessarily forceful tug can leave the nurse with a painful low back strain.

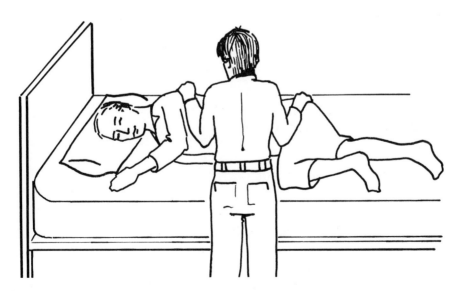

Fig. 34. Turning the Bed Patient

MAKING THE BED

Bed linen should be changed frequently; wet or soiled sheets must be replaced immediately. If repeated wetness is a problem, a rubber pad beneath the sheet avoids a soggy mattress. The linen should be kept smooth to prevent pressure sores.

To change sheets while the patient is still in bed, first loosen all the bedclothes at the edges. Turn the patient, as described in the last section, so that he is lying on his side on one half of the bed. Walk around to the empty side of the bed and roll the soiled undersheet lengthwise toward the patient. Place the clean sheet under the mattress and on top of the bed in the position it is to occupy. Push the unused half of the clean sheet toward the patient, then go to the opposite side of the bed and turn the patient to lie on the clean sheet. The soiled sheet is removed from the bed, and the unused half of the clean sheet is pulled toward you and tucked under the mattress to complete the change. The upper sheet and pillowcase are easily replaced.

FEEDING

The disabled elderly person should be placed in a comfortable position for the meal, in a chair or bed, with the back supported with several pillows. He should be fed at a table if sitting in a hard-backed chair, while the bedfast patient should be fed from a supported bedtray.

The patient may need help spreading butter or cutting meat; if he is unable to sit up, small amounts of solid food will be fed to him slowly. For drinking, the head should be raised and fluid offered from a cup or through a plastic straw between mouthfuls of solid food. Don't rush. Ample time should be allowed for feeding because, as Shakespeare observed, "Unquiet meals make ill digestions."

Some elderly persons cannot consume enough food in three meals a day for adequate nutrition, and between-meal feedings of juice, milk, or protein-enriched liquids may be necessary to provide fuel for energy and repairs. Vitamin supplements may be given at mealtimes.

Remember that, with the limited activities of the older person, mealtime is a focal point of the day. Strive to make dining a pleasant experience.

BATHING IN BED

The disabled elderly bedfast patient must be bathed in bed. The room must be warm to avoid chilling. A bedpan should be offered just prior to the bath; before beginning the bath, the patient's teeth should be brushed. Then the patient is completely disrobed and covered with a light bath blanket. All bedclothes except the bottom sheet should be removed, and a bath blanket is placed beneath the patient, using the technique described for making the bed.

The patient's body is washed area by area, each arm and each leg at a time, and dried before proceeding to the next area. The eyes are bathed with a washcloth and clear water, and the nails are cleaned and trimmed if needed. Skin folds and bony prominences of the body should receive special care at bath time, and the hair is carefully combed. An alcohol backrub followed with light dusting of talcum powder is refreshing.

The thorough daily bath allows regular inspection of the body for early signs of skin infections or ulcers.

ENEMAS

The normal bowel relies upon active body motion for much of its forward movement; with inactivity, bowel sluggishness leads to the discomfort of constipation. While much constipation can be prevented by adequate hydration and regular use of stool softeners, occasional severe episodes may occur in all but the most fortunate senior citizen. In very severe cases, enemas are necessary to prevent a fecal impaction—the formation of a painful dry hard mass of stool at the rectum, which must be broken up with the doctor's finger and removed with oil.

The conventional enema, using an enema bag and tubing, floods the rectum with tap water or weak soapsuds; any mild soap will do. One quart of solution is the usual amount used for an adult, and the solution should be slightly warmer than body temperature. The enema bag is held 12 inches above the rectum, trapped air is carefully bubbled from the tubing, and the rectal tip is gently inserted about three inches into the rectum. The enema solution is administered slowly, over a five-minute period of time, to prevent acute discomfort. If cramps occur, stop the flow temporarily by pinching off the tube.

The enema solution should be retained for five to ten minutes if possible. When administering an enema, it is necessary to have a bedpan or toilet nearby.

The advent of disposable products has simplified enema administration. The Fleet Company makes an excellent disposable enema contained in a plastic squeeze bottle with a lubricated rectal tip that sells for less than one dollar. The covering is removed, the rectal tip is inserted high in the rectum, and the enema is gently forced into the rectum by slowly squeezing the bottle. The enema solution is held as long as possible, ideally for five or ten minutes, when the enema and feces are expelled.

The Fleet Company also makes an oil enema helpful in removing fecal impactions. With proper diet, hydration, judicious use of laxatives and enemas, fecal impactions in the elderly patient should occur rarely.

BEDPANS

Bedpans are a necessary evil—cold, hard, awkward, and singularly lacking in dignity. All efforts should be made to find an alternative method for facilitating the evacuation of the bowels.

Sometimes, however, there is no choice; if so, the bedpan should be hard plastic rather than metal. Stainless steel is cold! When positioning the patient on the bedpan, he should be rolled to his side, using the maneuvers described earlier in this chapter. The bedpan is placed in position, and the patient is rolled back onto it. After the bowels have been evacuated, the rectum is wiped clean with toilet tissue, the bedpan is removed, and the patient is returned to his previous position. The bedpan is emptied, washed with hot tap water, and cleansed with alcohol.

Alternatives to the bedpan have been advised. The sanitary chair is a wheelchair with an ordinary toilet seat as the base. The bedpan may be placed underneath the toilet seat of the chair, or the sanitary chair may be wheeled into the bathroom over the toilet bowl. The use of the sanitary chair is a luxury compared to evacuating the bowels while lying in bed with the buttocks elevated awkwardly on a bedpan.

Another handy mechanical device is a toilet seat on a tubular framework. The toilet seat is positioned under the patient, and a pull on the handle raises the patient on the toilet seat six inches off the bed so that a bedpan may be placed under the device. A back rest is included in the framework so that the patient may evacuate the bowels in a sitting position.

Energy and motion studies have shown that using a bedpan is more strenuous for the patient than sitting on a toilet. Bedpans contribute to ulcers of the skin and heart attacks and may cause hernias and breakdown of surgical incisions. Try to find a satisfactory method of evacuation other than the bedpan.

RESTRAINTS

A wide variety of restraints have been used to prevent the patient from injuring himself or his attendants. Side rails on the bed are a form of restraint and should be employed for all persons in danger of falling out of bed. The chest restraint may be used with the patient lying in bed or sitting in a chair. A simple home chest restraint may be made by placing a single-size bed sheet across the patient's chest under the arms and pinning it under the mattress. Commercially manufactured chest restraints consist of a vest for the patient's chest with straps to go under the mattress or behind the back of the chair. Agitated, aggressive individuals may require wrist and ankle restraints, but shackles of this type should be reserved for institutional use. The need for restraints raises the question of the advisability of continuing home-nursing care.

WALKERS, CRUTCHES, AND CANES

Walkers, crutches, and canes, used by elderly persons who have difficulty in walking because of stroke, arthritis, and fracture, can be of inestimable value, and their use is often prescribed in a progressive manner. The stroke or hip-fracture victim, upon beginning ambulation, will make his debut on the parallel bars under the watchful eyes of a physical therapist. After mastering the parallel bars in the physical therapy department, the patient will be instructed in the use of a walker or crutches. Later, if there is sufficient strength in the involved limb, a cane may be prescribed.

Walkers have taken many forms over the years. One of the earliest walkers was a light kitchen chair pushed forward by elderly patients for support. Ingenious carpenters eventually devised the walker in the form it is used now, at first produced from wood and later manufactured in firm tubular steel with rubber handholds. The modern walker retains its earliest function, a support pushed ahead of the body with both hands, allowing the patient to lean on the walker while moving the weakened limb forward.

Walkers are useful for elderly patients, particularly hip-fracture victims who lack the muscular strength and coordination to use crutches. The use of a walker requires normal function in both arms and is therefore sometimes not practical for stroke victims.

Crutches, requiring a fair degree of muscular strength in the forearms, are most useful following fractures of the hip or leg. Because of the strength required, crutches are rarely used following a stroke or in the patient with arthritis of the wrist and hands.

Crutches must be carefully fitted so that the weight is borne on the forearms, avoiding underarm pressure that can damage nerves. Some instruction will be necessary before embarking on their use. Especially difficult is the descent of stairs, where the wrong maneuver can leave the patient swinging perilously out into space.

Canes, intended for less serious disabilities, aid balance and compensate for minor weakness of a leg. The cane should be carried in the hand opposite the injury. This allows the full weight to be put on the good leg; when the injured side is moved, half the weight goes on the cane and half on the injured side. Many stroke victims have been helped by the use of a tripod cane, a tubular steel cane with a three-point base that aids in stability.

Although many older persons will require the use of a walker, crutch, or cane for a prolonged period of time, the senior citizen has crossed the goal line when he can discard these appliances and walk proudly on his own two feet.

Special Problems
of the
Elderly

Disease has nothing refined about it,
nothing dignified
THOMAS MANN
(1875-1955)

INDWELLING CATHETER

An indwelling catheter in the bladder is sometimes a necessary evil. The patient who is incontinent of urine will be found frequently lying in a pool as the odor of stale urine pervades the room. Urine breaks down the protective layers of skin as does a diaper rash in babies; if the irritation persists, infection and bedsores soon follow.

Senile individuals with advanced chronic brain deterioration may lose voluntary control and pass urine unconsciously. Diabetics whose disease has been present for a long time may suffer short-circuited nerves to the bladder and consequent loss of urinary control. Older women with damage of the bladder support and elderly men with enlarged prostates whose general health does not permit surgical repair may require catheterization to allow passage of urine. The use of a catheter in the bladder may be temporary in conditions such as a stroke or a fractured hip, where removal of the catheter is another milestone on the road to recovery, or may be permanent when chronic brain damage dashes all hope of improvement.

The home care of an indwelling catheter can be difficult. Before embarking upon a course in catheter maintenance, one should make every effort to effect surgical or medical correction of the underlying condition. Since a catheter in the bladder often causes infection in the urinary tract, catheters must be changed at regular intervals of two to three weeks. The indwelling catheter may irritate the wall of the bladder, producing bleeding, and blood clots, or the accumulation of urinary sediment may block the catheter, causing severe and painful bladder spasms.

In spite of its many disadvantages, the home use of an indwelling catheter may spell the difference between grandfather's living in his own room or in a nursing home bed. The actual insertion of the urinary catheter should be left to the doctor or nurse. Indeed, if a catheter is to be left in place, a public health nurse should visit regularly to oversee its maintenance. The physician may prescribe daily doses of a sulfonamide or Hiprex to minimize the chance of bladder infection.

After insertion, the draining end of the catheter will be fitted to a collecting tube that runs into a container; a one-gallon cider jug is useful. If the person is able to be out of bed and walking, the collecting tube is fitted to a Bardex bag strapped to the leg, allowing the patient to walk from room to room with the catheter in place.

Catheters must be irrigated regularly, preferably every two to three days, to wash out sediment that may block the passage. The most useful solution for irrigation is sterile distilled water, available at the local pharmacy. A one-pint stainless steel or plastic basin will be needed, as well as a large irrigating syringe with a rubber bulb. Cleanliness is important; careless irrigation can cause a bladder infection. The technique of bladder irrigation is as follows. The sterile basin is filled with sterile distilled water. The irrigating syringe is filled from the basin and is inserted in the catheter opening. The distilled water in the syringe is expelled into the bladder and then withdrawn into the syringe and discarded. The syringe is refilled, and the bladder reirrigated five or six times until the return in the syringe is clean. Then the catheter is reattached to the drainage tube, and the irrigation instruments are sterilized.

Normal urination without a catheter should always be the goal. Bladder training consists of clamping the catheter for progressively longer periods over several weeks. As the catheter is clamped and the bladder fills, the patient reports when he first feels the urge to void. Some individuals fail to feel the urge to void, even when the bladder contains a quart of urine; these patients are not candidates for catheter removal. Other individuals will sense a normal urge to void when the bladder contains about one and a half cups of urine, justifying an attempt at catheter removal.

COLOSTOMY

A colostomy, the surgical creation of an opening by which the colon exits through the abdominal wall, may be a temporary measure, seen as the first stage in the repair of an intestinal obstruction or tumor when the large intestine is too stretched and inflamed to allow the extensive surgical repair that will be done later. More commonly, however, the colostomy opening is a permanent fixture, with operative closure of the rectum. Colostomies are usually the result of the extensive surgery necessary for cure of carcinoma of the rectum and should be regarded as a fair exchange for the cure of a cancer.

The colostomy incision represents an artificial anus on the abdominal wall; however, it lacks the normal anal muscles that control feces and thus will discharge feces at capricious times unless controlled by irrigation. Some colostomy patients prefer to wear a bag strapped to the abdomen at all times. However, more fastidious people prefer to irrigate the colostomy area daily and between irrigations need only wear a four-inch-square gauze pad over the opening.

With the approval of the attending physician, the nurse should instruct the patient in proper irrigation before he is discharged to home care. The colostomy patient should be visited by his physician regularly and by the public health nurse frequently.

One technique of colostomy irrigation with the bulb syringe is as follows. The patient sits straddling the toilet facing the toilet tank (see Figure 35). (Patients unable to assume this position may receive their irrigations in bed, although this is less handy.) An 18-inch disposable plastic drainage sheath is used to direct the flow of the irrigated material down into the toilet. The sheath is attached to a colostomy ring that adapts to the colostomy opening and is held in place by an elastic belt encircling the waist. While the patient straddles the toilet and with the drainage sheath in place, a small opening is cut in the sheath near the colostomy opening to allow the introduction of the syringe tip into the colostomy.

An 8-ounce rubber bulb syringe with a flexible tip is filled with warm water. The flexible tip is lubricated with standard lubricating jelly and is inserted through the hole in the drainage sheath into the colostomy about four inches. With gentle pressure, a steady stream of

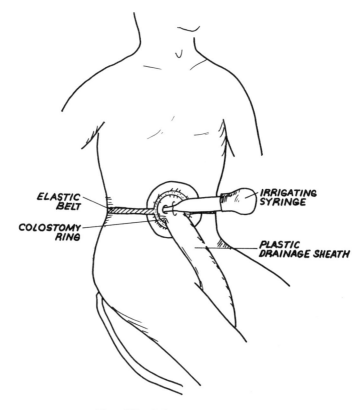

ELASTIC BELT

COLOSTOMY RING

IRRIGATING SYRINGE

PLASTIC DRAINAGE SHEATH

Fig. 35. Colostomy Irrigation

water is expelled into the colostomy area until the syringe is empty. Only two or three syringefuls of water should be used during an irrigation—16 to 24 ounces.

After removal of the syringe tip, the colostomy will drain the water and feces down the drainage sheath into the toilet. The purpose of irrigation is to stimulate peristaltic action of the large intestine rather than mechanical flushing of the colon.

Following the evacuation of drainage fluid and feces, a standard colostomy bag is attached to the belt and worn for about 30 minutes while the last few ounces of fluid drain. Drainage should then be complete, and the patient may remove the colostomy bag and belt, covering the opening with three layers of four-inch-square gauze held in place with a nonirritating adhesive tape. The colostomy site must be irrigated daily to maintain regular bowel movements.

Although most long-term colostomy patients require few dietary restrictions, the following diet has been useful in the initial management of the colostomy.

COLOSTOMY DIET

Soups:	All soups, except those containing beans, corn, or tomato extract
Bread and Cereal:	Cooked cereal, white bread, and saltines
Fruits:	Any cooked or canned fruit, fruit juice
Meat and Fish:	Beef, lamb, veal, turkey, chicken, and fish
Vegetables:	Cooked string beans, carrots, squash, beets, asparagus, cauliflower, peas, lettuce, and celery
	Baked or mashed potato, rice
Cheese:	Cottage cheese, mild cheddar cheese
Beverages:	Milk, tea, cocoa, coffee
Desserts:	Custard, gelatin, angel cake, sponge cake, soft puddings
Miscellaneous:	Macaroni, spaghetti, noodles
	Butter or margarine
	Salt in moderation
	Sugar in moderation

TUBE FEEDING

Extremely debilitated persons will often be unable to consume food by mouth. Intravenous feeding is impracticable for more than several weeks, and tube feeding becomes the only method of maintaining nutrition. Tube feeding involves the passage of a nasogastric tube through the nose and down the throat into the stomach. The proper technique of nasogastric tube feeding requires the passage of the tube with each feeding, since a tube left in place may damage the membranes of the nose, throat, and stomach. The feeding tube is usually passed twice daily; a rubber bulb syringe introduces the food through the tube and into the stomach. Nasogastric tube feeding is a hospital or nursing home procedure requiring skill and patience and should be attempted at home only by those trained in its use.

While a number of expensive synthetic formulas are available in the drugstore, the same nutritional value is obtained with the normal geriatric diet (see page 184), adding milk to increase the fluid content and homogenizing the mixture in a blender to produce a liquid that will pass through the tube. Any necessary pills may be crushed and mixed with the dinner, obviating the need for injections. Since the tube-fed patient is receiving exactly the same diet, vitamins, and medication as the patient able to eat from a plate, good nutrition can be maintained indefinitely.

BEDSORES

A bedsore is an ulceration of the skin caused by pressure while lying in bed. It occurs over bony prominences, usually the base of the spine, the hips, or the heels—those areas that bear the bulk of weight when reclining. Irritation begins as a slight redness of the skin and, if untreated, progresses to ulceration with a break in the outer layer of the skin. Infection may form, but the chief factor in bedsores is constant pressure.

Bedsores, preventable if anticipated and if precautions are taken to prevent their occurrence, are grim testimony to a failure of nursing care. Frequent changes of the patient's position—from his back to his side and then to his back again—are the chief defense against bedsores; if skin irritation over a bony prominence threatens, this change of position every two hours will be continued even through the night. Incontinence of urine or feces will break down skin as readily as heat melts butter and must be corrected, whether by an indwelling catheter or frequent enemas to keep the bowel empty. Wrinkles in the bedclothes can contribute to bedsores. Patients requiring prolonged confinement to bed may use an air mattress with a pump that constantly changes the contour of the surface by filling and emptying small air tubes.

Bedsores are treated by preventing weight from bearing on the ulcerated area. An ingenious array of devices is available to minimize pressure on various parts of the body. Foam rubber cuffs around the ankles can keep ulcerated heels off the bed with complete comfort to the patient. A sheepskin pad under the buttocks minimizes pressure on the lower back and helps banish bedsores. More expensive is the water bed, a mattress filled with fluid that gives to fit the contour of the patient and spreads his weight evenly over the bearing surface. Moist ulcerations are dried with the careful use of a heat lamp. Bedsores full of old dead tissue are trimmed surgically, and Elase ointment is applied. For infected bedsores, antibiotic powders such as Neosporin or Furacin may be applied three times a day.

When You Need a Nursing Home

A lady with a lamp shall stand
In the great history of the land,
A noble type of good,
Heroic womanhood
HENRY WADSWORTH LONGFELLOW
(1807-1882)

IS A NURSING HOME NECESSARY?

Not everyone can handle a disabled elderly person at home. Even with a spare bedroom, nearby toilet, and the will to help, the physical condition of the patient may dictate his placement in a nursing home. An indwelling catheter is very difficult to manage at home without special training; stubborn bedsores may require several months of institutional therapy for cure; and tube feeding is a nursing procedure that should rarely be attempted in the home. A confused and agitated senile person will require the special care that can be found only in a nursing home.

The question, "Is nursing home care necessary?" is being asked by the Federal government with increasing frequency. Unfortunately, press releases concerning the Medicare law have led elderly persons and their families to believe that unlimited nursing home use is available to all persons over 65. Some elderly persons have budgeted their pennies, intending to spend their declining years in a nursing home under the

197

Medicare law, only to discover that Medicare will underwrite nursing home care only in certain cases, and then only for a limited period of time. Although nursing home operators are careful to explain these facts to families, it has been difficult to correct misconceptions of Medicare.

After admission to the nursing home (or extended care facility, the term preferred by Medicare representatives), the nursing home director and doctor must send reports to the area Medicare agency, where the information is evaluated by a Medicare representative, who decides whether nursing home care is necessary. If the Medicare representative decrees that nursing home care is not necessary within the narrow concept of the law, the government will refuse to pay for any part of the nursing home stay. Unfortunately, these determinations of necessity are usually made after the patient is admitted to the nursing home; by the time the Medicare representative has announced that it will not be responsible for payment, a sizable bill has already been incurred.

WHAT TO LOOK FOR IN A NURSING HOME

Across the United States, there were in 1973 more than 22,000 nursing homes, comprising more than 1,000,000 patient beds. A large number of these nursing homes have been built within the last decade in anticipation of receiving Federal funds through the Medicare and Medicaid programs. The newer nursing homes have been built to rigid Federal guidelines and offer a dramatic contrast to the old converted Victorian home that was the prototype of nursing homes until 1965.

Unfortunately, nursing homes have been a favorite target of publicity-seeking politicians and editors. Exposés in magazines have capitalized on a few unfortunate episodes in isolated institutions. The vast majority of nursing homes are operated by conscientious capable persons who try to provide the best possible medical care to all their patients. A frank discussion with the nursing home administrator or head nurse should convince you of their professional dedication.

Before deciding upon a nursing home, you should visit the facility at least once. Admitting an elderly relative to a nursing home is a major step in his life, and a careful decision is in order. Upon entering, stop inside the door and look around. Is the hallway wide and inviting? Is there adequate ventilation and light? Is the home air conditioned? Are there unpleasant odors? Do patients wander about aimlessly, or do they seem to have purposeful activity? Is there an air of cheerfulness or does gloom hang like ether in the air?

Ask to speak to the administrator or head nurse. You should discuss the philosophy of the nursing home and the type of care it is designed to provide. Some nursing homes are little more than rest homes with a nurse on duty to dispense medication, but top-flight nursing homes are really extensions of hospital care—hence the term extended care facility. There should be a dietitian to implement the doctor's diet prescription. A physical therapist should be available daily to carry out the doctor's therapy orders, plus a treatment room with parallel bars, a large wall wheel to exercise shoulders, and an assortment of canes, crutches, and walkers. There may be a whirlpool bath, and there should be a means of applying heat such as diathermy, hot packs, or ultrasound. A recreation therapist should have adequate facilities and equipment at her disposal, including those for leatherwork, knitting, sewing, and painting. There should be a cheerful solarium for relaxation, card games, chess, and checkers. The nursing home may have a social worker to assist the senior citizens in their dealings with Social Security, the county social service agencies, and pension funds, as well as in dealing with lawyers, taxes, and insurance companies.

Notice the patients you see. In any nursing home, the patients will range from ambulatory elderly persons dressed in street clothes to comatose bedfast individuals kept alive by a network of tubes. A nursing home where all the patients are up and about indicates a low level of medical care and might be poorly equipped to handle acute illness. A nursing home where most of the patients are bedfast, requiring intensive nursing care with tubes, catheters, and intravenous feedings, might raise the question, "Does father really need a nursing home providing such a high and expensive level of nursing care?"

Peek at the trays coming from the kitchen. Is the food appetizing and tastefully served? Don't expect steak and rib roast; the elderly patient needs a soft bland diet. Does the nurse check to see that all patients consume a reasonable portion of their dinner?

Survey the rooms. Are they equipped with modern hospital beds and siderails or do the beds look like cast-off camp furniture? Is there a buzzer system so that the nurse can be summoned in an emergency? Are the rooms clean and airy? Are a closet and bureau available? Is there adequate light in the room? Is a private toilet available, with a hand grip on the wall to prevent falls? If a private toilet is not available, how close and how crowded are the nearest toilet facilities?

Even if you do not intend to request Medicare assistance, ask if the nursing home is accredited for Medicare payments. Nursing homes with Medicare accreditation must meet rigid inspection standards. Medicare inspectors examine aspects of the nursing home, such as medical records, doctor's orders, and fireproofing, to which you would not have access.

After evaluating the rooms, diet, and nursing care, you must ask yourself the question, "Will my relative be happy living here?" If the answer is yes and your relative agrees, then you will probably be satisfied with your choice of a nursing home.

THE NURSING HOME DOCTOR

After admission to the nursing home, a disabled elderly person requires medical care. If you are fortunate in having a qualified nursing home in your home town, then your relative's personal physician will want to continue his medical care at the nursing home. State and Federal laws require that nursing home patients receive regular medical attention. In New York State, the patient newly admitted to the nursing home must give his complete medical history and have a physical examination within 48 hours. Extensive reports must be filed, both for the nursing home records and with Medicare. Medicare suggests a regular monthly examination, with appropriate progress notes on the record, but more frequent checkups will be provided if the patient's condition requires them.

In most cases, the nursing home will be some distance from your residence, and your regular physician will be unable to continue medical care. The nursing home will have a panel of doctors composed of local practitioners prepared to care for nursing home patients. The home administrator will furnish you with the names of doctors on his panel and assist you in making a choice. The physician you choose will visit the nursing home within a day or two after the patient's arrival and perform the necessary examination.

The nursing home doctor has responsibility for medical care for your aged disabled relative while he is in the nursing home. This physician will be your best source of information because nursing home personnel may not divulge detailed information about the patient. After his initial examination, you should call the doctor to introduce yourself and ask about his findings. As the months go by, you should call the doctor regularly to obtain progress reports and you should request him to notify you at any time if there is any sudden change in condition. The doctor should have available an alternate telephone number, perhaps that of your office or a relative, in case you are not at home when he calls.

The nursing home physician will send a monthly statement of his professional fees. Medicare extended-care benefits in the nursing home (Part A) do not cover the services of the nursing home physician, although Part B may cover some portion of his professional fees. While some doctors will accept Medicare assignments for services rendered in the nursing home, because of uncertainties in Medicare collections, many physicians will bill the patient or family directly for services rendered, offering assistance in filling out Medicare forms to help recover that portion of his fee that Medicare will allow.

CAN WE AFFORD A NURSING HOME?

Nursing homes are expensive. Nursing home fees range from $20 per day for a semiprivate room with a modest level of nursing care to $40 per day or more for a private room with skilled nursing. Nursing homes that charge less than $20 per day cannot afford to provide adequate nursing services.

The extended-care benefits of the Medicare program will subsidize nursing home treatment in certain limited instances. Extended care refers to nursing home treatment that is an extension of therapy begun in the hospital. Medicare will pay part or all of the extended-care nursing home therapy if the following provisions are met:

1. The extended-care services must be "medically necessary" as defined by Medicare's interpretation of rigid criteria. The care required for an indwelling catheter or a colostomy, severe debility, or mental confusion *will not necessarily* qualify a patient for extended-care benefits. The factor most likely to qualify a patient for Medicare approval is a plan of treatment, such as physical therapy, expected to effect substantial improvement in the patient's condition.

2. The patient must have been hospitalized for at least three consecutive days and must be admitted to the nursing home within 14 days after discharge from the hospital.

3. The admission to the nursing home must be for extended care of a condition for which the patient was treated in the hospital.

The extended-care benefits program of Medicare will pay for the following services in the nursing home:

1. A semiprivate room (two to four beds) and all meals, including a special diet prescribed by the doctor, plus a supplemental payment for a private room if the patient's medical condition requires it.

2. All drugs prescribed while in the nursing home.

3. Such appliances as splints, casts, wheelchairs, and walkers.

4. Physical, speech, and occupational therapy.

5. Nursing and social services.

Extended-care benefits of the Medicare program do not pay for:

1. Physician's services under Part A. However, Part B will cover some portion of this charge.

2. Convenience items such as a telephone.

3. The extra charge for a private room, unless medically necessary.

4. Private duty nurses.

The Medicare law permits a maximum extended-care period of 100 days, with full payment for the first 20 days and coverage for all but $9 per day for the next 80 days. In practice, however, the regional agencies administering Medicare usually disallow treatment many weeks before the 100-day period has expired; once Medicare benefits have expired, the full nursing home charges become the responsibility of the patient and his family. If the 100-day extended-care benefits period has expired, the patient must have received home care (that is, not as a patient in a hospital or another nursing home) for 60 days before he is again eligible for another 100-day period of extended-care benefits.

You may say that the foregoing is fine for relatively wealthy persons, but wonder about the retired worker who, at 75, has only a few dollars in the bank and a small pension and whose family cannot afford $35 a day for a nursing home after Medicare benefits cease.

Older persons whose modest finances prevent private payment of nursing home fees and whose Medicare benefits have expired or been denied can obtain nursing home care in the following way: Apply to the county social service office for Medicaid. Each county has a number of Medicaid nursing home beds available. Before filling in the obligatory form stating financial assets, find out the criteria for Medicaid eligibility; these vary in different localities. Representative requirements are as follows:

1. The patient may own his home wholly or in part.

2. He must not have more than $2,000 in savings accounts or cash value of life insurance.

3. He must not have pension or Social Security income of more than $180 per month.

If assets exceed local criteria, the patient can qualify for Medicaid only by divesting himself of his money. He may consult a lawyer or mortician about a burial trust or make gifts to minor children or grandchildren. Alternatively, admit your father to a nursing home and spend his money for necessary care until his assets drop to the predetermined level, when Medicaid will cover all future nursing home care. There is no time limit to Medicaid benefits; once qualified, the patient can remain in the nursing home at Medicaid expense indefinitely.

Medicare and Medicaid money is available to pay for nursing home care for those who lack the funds to pay their own way. However, be prepared for red tape, letter writing, and sometimes a formal hearing to obtain legislated benefits. With proper medical and legal advice, the benefits of nursing home care should be available to all American senior citizens regardless of income.

The Senior Citizen Enters the Hospital

Life is a hospital in which every patient
is possessed by the desire to change his bed.
CHARLES BAUDELAIRE
(1821-1867)

YOUR PERSONAL PHYSICIAN

Sooner or later, most senior citizens must enter the hospital, perhaps following a stroke, heart attack, or fractured hip. Usually the patient will be examined at home or in the office by the physician, who will arrange for admission to the hospital. The family doctor is a free agent, permitted to practice medicine in the hospital by satisfying specific requirements of professional training. To keep his hospital privileges, the doctor must agree to abide by certain hospital rules and broad concepts of medical ethics. His first responsibility, however, is to the patient.

Upon the patient's admission to the hospital, the doctor is responsible for literally everything that happens. He orders the diet, medication, and physical therapy; if the room seems noisy or crowded, the doctor will try to arrange for transfer to another. Any necessary consultation with a specialist will be arranged by the personal physician, and surgery will not be undertaken without his approval.

If several specialists and therapists participate in the patient's care, the family may wonder where responsibility rests. The family physician's duty, even in complex cases beyond the scope of his training, is to assign responsibility for all phases of treatment and keep the lines of communication open to the patient's family. The patient's family should feel free to call the family physician at any reasonable time for progress reports and reassurance.

THE HOSPITAL HIERARCHY

When the gears mesh smoothly, the patient and his family should not be aware of the hospital hierarchy: the structured division of responsibility within the institution. Individuals with authority higher than that of your personal physician should be contacted only if a serious difficulty arises. However, if a problem is not promptly settled to your satisfaction, don't hesitate to call upon the appropriate hospital officer.

Every hospital has a board of directors; although they may vary in title and number, their function is to lay the basic foundation of hospital policy. The board of directors is usually composed of leading citizens in the community who meet at regular intervals to consider problems referred to them by the hospital administrator, medical director, community representatives, or patients. A personal complaint should be referred to the hospital board of directors only after all other sources of satisfaction have been exhausted.

The hospital administrator oversees all employees of the hospital except the physicians; he carries the responsibility for maintenance, housekeeping, the dietary, nursing, and social services, the business and admissions offices, medical records, and grounds. Serving under the hospital administrator are the head janitor, the head housekeeper, the dietitian, the director of nursing services, the medical records librarian, the social worker, and other department heads.

The medical director, the senior physician in the hospital, is official head of the medical staff. His is either a salaried position or an honorary one, with voluntary assumption of responsibility. Under the leadership of the medical director, the medical staff will be divided into departments of surgery, internal medicine, pediatrics, family practice, pathology, radiology, and others. Each medical division will have an elected head or chief, who makes administrative decisions within his department. Your family doctor will be a member of one of these departments, very likely the department of family practice, and consultants will belong to one of the other divisions, such as the department of internal medicine or surgery.

The hospital hierarchy becomes important in a crisis. Perhaps your father is placed in a room with a confused aggressive patient; his room may be near a noisy nurses' station; his quarters may be roasting in the summer and frost may form on the bedpan in winter. Roast beef may be as tender as an old wallet, and the chicken soup may taste as though the bird had expired of natural causes. There may be a personality clash with a floor nurse, a complaint about a surly aide, or a question concerning an apparently illiterate clerk. All problems should first be discussed with your family doctor, who will solve all but the thorniest. A change of room, a call to the dietitian, or a word to the chief of maintenance may be all that is needed to change frowns to smiles.

If, however, the attending physician is unable to solve the problem it's time to call on the medical director or the hospital administrator. You will find both of these men interested in the patients' welfare and vitally aware of the hospital's image in the community. Usually a brief phone call from their offices can solve a difficult problem.

Hospital employees, from the board of directors to the housekeeper, work hard, often harder than their counterparts in industry. Double shifts and overloaded work schedules are common. If you are impressed by the dedication of the personnel with whom you come in contact, it takes only a few seconds to write a brief thank-you note to the nurse or aide involved. Another note to the hospital administrator may be the bright spot of his day.

THE HOSPITAL DAY

The hospital day begins early. At seven o'clock in the morning the hall lights go on and the night nurses are replaced by the day shift. Since most nursing procedures are carried out during the day, the day shift will be larger and have more responsibilities than the night crew. If the doctor has ordered blood tests or X rays, a small flag may wave at the foot of the bed to alert the kitchen to hold breakfast until all procedures have been completed. Early morning medications often arrive before breakfast, and a therapist often appears at the bedside before the morning coffee cools.

X rays are usually performed in the morning, particularly such extensive procedures as X rays of the stomach, gallbladder, kidneys, and intestines. Surgery begins early, usually about eight o'clock to avoid keeping the patient waiting anxiously. The doctor usually makes his rounds in the morning, reviewing tests performed on the previous day, checking progress, and planning procedures for tomorrow.

Following lunch, the less complicated X rays, such as those of the chest, arm, and leg, are performed. An electrocardiogram may be taken, or the patient may visit physical therapy for treatment. Visiting hours begin, and as the afternoon progresses, the hospital procedures for the day are completed. Following dinner, there will be a large influx of visitors, who will be allowed to stay until perhaps eight o'clock; later, following their departure, the evening medications are passed out to the patients. Laxatives are given if necessary, and the patient is offered a sleeping pill if needed. Lights may be turned out between nine and ten o'clock, and the only sound may be the nurse's quiet footsteps as she checks her sleeping charges.

During the hospital day, the patient meets three different shifts of nurses, each under the direction of a head nurse, who has responsibility for the activities of the floor during her period. I have often told patients that their experience in the hospital will be as good or as bad as the head nurse on the floor. Once she has attained the position of head nurse, the R. N. frequently retains it for many years. A hospital floor will eventually take on the personality of the day shift's charge nurse, whether punctual, compulsive, cheerful, or condescending. All comments concerning procedures on the floor should be directed to the head nurse and to your private physician.

WHAT CAN I DO TO HELP?

When an elderly family member enters the hospital, the family often asks the doctor, "What can I do to help?" While the direction of medical care will be under the supervision of the physician, the family can do a great deal to speed recovery.

The elderly patient entering the hospital often feels a sense of impending doom. Younger persons have grown up with a factual acceptance of hospital care, readily entering hospitals for appendectomy, hernia repair, childbirth, or even overwhelming flu. Many senior citizens, however, were reared in an era when one entered the hospital only to die! Admission to the hospital often challenges the senior citizen with the possibility of death.

The hospital days may be long and tedious. Frequent reminders that the patient is important to those at home help brighten the day. A basket of fruit or a bouquet of flowers shows the senior citizen that he has not been forgotten. A favorite book may be brought when visiting, and a radio or small portable television set may be allowed. Make sure your elderly parent's friends realize that he's in the hospital so that they may send cards and letters. If the illness is severe, perhaps distant relatives should be notified. Servicemen may be brought home from abroad in critical cases.

Visitors should be cautioned to keep their sessions brief; about 15 minutes is adequate for a good visit. The ill should not be expected to entertain. Visitors should discuss only constructive ideas and not regale the patient with sad tales of their own ailments or of turmoil at home. Gifts of sweets give dietitians grey hair and should be discouraged. Be sure that visitors do not bring colds or flu as "gifts" for the already ailing patient.

You and your physician should discuss progress regularly. Remember that the doctor, who sees his patient only a few minutes each day, is not in the hospital to observe what goes on at other times. Perhaps a portable toilet could be used instead of a bedpan, but with complicated tests and procedures, no one has thought to order this simple convenience. Perhaps the patient is allowed out of bed too long and is overtired by suppertime or is very restless in the afternoon and needs a mild tranquilizer. Maybe the patient is ready for physical therapy twice a day instead of once. Possibly the kitchen is serving the toothless oldster corn on the cob or the diabetic chocolate cake. The family doctor needs to know these facts; if a change in the routine is necessary, he will see that it is made. With the cooperation of the doctor, the hospital staff, and a devoted family, the patient has the best possible chance for a swift return home.

WHAT YOU CAN EXPECT FROM MEDICARE

Upon placing an elder family member in the hospital, you will become responsible for two payments: the hospital bill and the doctor bill. Medicare Part A will pay almost all of the hospital bill if care is rendered at a participating hospital. Under Part B, Medicare will pay or reimburse you for most of your doctor fees.

Part A of Medicare covers a broad range of services. Upon entering the hospital, the patient is responsible for the first $72.00 of charges (effective January 1, 1973), and this amount is subject to revision yearly. After the $72.00 deductible has been met, Medicare should completely cover the cost of the first 60 days of hospitalization, with a few exceptions that will be mentioned. During the next 30 hospital days, Medicare will allow all but $18.00 each day. After the patient has been in the hospital for 90 days, the Medicare responsibility for that period ends. The patient becomes eligible for another 90 days of hospital care when he has been out of a hospital or extended-care facility for 60 consecutive days. Once during his lifetime, the patient may call upon a lifetime reserve of 60 days of additional hospitalization, during which time he is responsible for half of the current hospital deductible ($36.00 at press time) for each day of the lifetime reserve used.

Thus, Mr. Jones may enter the hospital and be discharged in about three weeks. After a few days at home, Mr. Jones is readmitted to the hospital and continues within the same 90-day benefit period covered during the first hospitalization. If, however, he has been at home for more than 60 days, readmission to the hospital begins a new benefit period. There is no limit to the number of benefit periods a senior citizen may have during his lifetime.

Part A of Medicare includes payment for the following while the patient is in an approved hospital:

1. Medicare covers a semi-private hospital room (2 to 4 beds) and all meals, including special diets. The additional charge for a private room must be borne by the patient unless the physician certifies the medical necessity for such isolation.

2. Medicare pays for operating room charges and fees for intensive care nursing.

3. Medicare covers drugs, X rays, and laboratory tests provided by the hospital.

4. Medicare covers splints, casts, equipment, and appliances furnished by the hospital.

5. Part A of Medicare helps pay for medical social services.

Part A of Medicare will *not* pay for the following:

1. Medicare does not cover physician's services.

2. Items for personal convenience such as a telephone in the room are not covered.

3. Medicare does not cover pay for private-duty nurses.

Part B of Medicare covers services of physicians, certain dental surgery, ambulance, outpatient X ray, and laboratory services. Under Part B, payment will be made to the doctor or the patient for 80 per cent of the "allowed charges" incurred during a calendar year after the first $60.00 has been deducted. Thus, the accumulated doctor bills for the calendar year, when submitted to Medicare, will first be reduced to the level of charges in the Medicare fee schedule. The Medicare fee schedule, devised when Medicare was enacted several years ago, has been "frozen" since 1971. The office expenses of the physician, however, have not been frozen, and, as his costs have skyrocketed, fees have risen to levels above the Medicare schedule. Nevertheless, your physician's fee will be reduced to conform to the older Medicare schedule.

Next, Medicare will deduct the first $60.00 in charges, and no payment will be made for that amount. Finally, the Medicare computer will determine 80 per cent of the remaining figure, and this amount will be paid to you or your doctor.

There are two ways to receive Medicare benefits. If the doctor will accept assignment, he takes responsibility for filling in the Medicare form and will collect his fee directly from Medicare. In accepting assignment, the physician agrees to accept the Medicare fee determination as his total fee, and bills the patient for the first $60.00, plus the 20 per cent coinsurance amount. Surgeons performing major operations, with $300 and $500 fees, frequently accept Medicare as full payment; the large surgical fee allows them to write off the portion denied by Medicare.

Other physicians elect not to accept Medicare assignment. These physicians bill the patient directly and, toward the end of the calendar year, assist the patient in filling in a Medicare form so that the patient or his family receives reimbursement. Many family physicians bill the patient directly, because of the voluminous paper work involved in collecting single office charges, capricious fee reductions by Medicare, and a feeling that the payment of a modest office fee allows the patient the dignity of knowing that he is not a charity case. The year-end computation covering a large number of office calls during the year is made by the Medicare computer; all fees are reduced to the meager Medicare fee schedule, $60.00 is deducted, and payment is made for 80 per cent of the balance.

Part B of Medicare covers the following services:

1. Medicare covers most medical and surgical services by a physician, as well as certain surgical care provided by the dentist or podiatrist.

2. Medicare covers outpatient laboratory, and X-ray services.

3. Medicare covers ambulance service, provided the physician certifies that the ambulance services were necessary.

4. Medicare will help pay for surgical dressings, casts, and corrective lenses after cataract surgery.

5. Medicare helps pay for home nursing service, physical therapy, and occupational and speech therapy on a part-time basis.

Part B of Medicare does *not* cover the following:

1. Medicare does not cover routine physical checkups, foot care, eye refractions, or hearing tests; prophylactic immunizations such as flu shots are also excluded.

2. Medicare does not pay for medications that can be taken at home.

3. Medicare does not cover services of certain practitioners, such as Christian Science practitioners or naturopaths.

4. Medicare does not pay for hearing aids, eyeglasses, false teeth, or orthopedic shoes (unless attached to a leg brace).

It is your physician's prerogative to decide whether he will accept payment directly from Medicare or bill you directly. Whether or not he accepts direct payment, your doctor or his secretary should assist you with the preparation of the necessary form to obtain your legal benefits under the Medicare law.

Death, the Last Chapter

The old order changeth, yielding place to new,
And God fulfills himself in many ways. . .
LORD ALFRED TENNYSON
(1809-1892)

THE FLAME OF HOPE BURNS ON

I know a great physician who has grown old with his patients. He has helped many of them through their last days, finding countless hours to sit with the dying patient and his family. He patiently answers their questions and calms their anxieties. Although the patient and his family are aware of the likelihood of death, this doctor avoids the despair of finality. I have never heard him utter a death judgment. He allows the patient to hope!

The patient is allowed to hope that a course of chemical therapy may arrest the disease, at least temporarily, or that X-ray treatments may cause a remission. The family is reassured that everything possible is being done for the patient, and they are encouraged to radiate an attitude of hope.

FAMILY MEMBERS SHOULD BE PREPARED

Although few are ever really resigned, the impact of death's dread scythe is eased when family members have been forewarned of its coming. When serious illness strikes an elder family member, the physician should be specifically questioned as to the likelihood of death.

If your elderly relative's condition is deteriorating, you should be in frequent contact with the physician. A responsible member of the family should be delegated to contact the physician daily or as often as necessary, reporting to others in the family any change in the condition. It will be the responsibility of the family delegate to decide what information should be passed to which members of the household. Perhaps an elderly grandmother should not be told all the grim details of her husband's condition; certainly young children should be spared the agonies of impending death.

HOW MUCH SHOULD THE PATIENT BE TOLD?

The family must carefully consider the response of the patient to information about his condition. The strong self-reliant man is often best informed of the outlook, even in the gravest conditions; there are matters that require his attention. Other more dependent personalities should be given less information. While the family physician should be consulted for his advice concerning the information to be given to the patient, the final decision must rest with the family.

COMMUNICATE WITH YOUR DOCTOR

When serious illness strikes an older person, the outlook changes from day to day. Your physician will be in constant touch with the hospital, receiving reports from the nurses and laboratory. The probability that death will occur may change from hour to hour.

Your family physician may be counted upon to inform you when death is imminent. However, with a busy practice, the physician may be unable to take the initiative to call and report each downward step of the patient's progress. Remember that hospital nurses are allowed to describe the patient's condition only in general terms, such as critical, serious, or satisfactory, and are forbidden to discuss details, even with the family. Therefore, the interested family must call upon the physician for up-to-the-minute information.

THE PROLONGATION OF LIFE

As death approaches, you should discuss with your physician his philosophy concerning the prolongation of life. If your death were inevitable, would you wish your life artificially prolonged by blood transfusions, a resuscitator, or medication to lift the blood pressure artificially?

If you feel that the use of heroic measures to prolong life artificially is unwarranted, you should communicate these views to your physician. You will probably find that he agrees, but perhaps hesitated to discuss this with the family of a dying patient. Everything possible should be done to maintain the nutrition and comfort of the terminal patient. Pain killers such as morphine should not be spared, sedatives should be administered whenever necessary, cortisone may give the dying patient a sense of well-being through the last few days, and oxygen may ease labored breathing. All these measures are intended to ease suffering during the last few days and hours of life.

EXAMINE YOUR FEELINGS

The death of a beloved family member can dredge to the surface emotions that have long been submerged beneath a sea of apparent tranquility. When life flows smoothly, we contain our feelings of guilt and jealousy, but in times of acute stress, such as death, repressed emotions rise to the surface. The most common emotion felt at the time of death is guilt! The children of an aged parent feel guilty that they did not write more often, that they did not spend enough time with him, or that there was not enough room in their home to accommodate him during his last few years. There are fantasies that the parent has been rejected. Guilt feelings, often with the flimsiest foundation, can sink the family of a dying patient into deep depression.

The death of an elder family member may bring out jealousies among the children. One child, who has chafed under the burden of supporting an aged parent, may feel that another did not contribute his share. The presence of an estate to be settled and heirlooms to be divided may well fan the flames of resentment.

Given adequate information concerning the probability of death, relatives can begin to work out their guilt feelings. The sudden trip to the bedside of a loved one helps to assuage the feelings of guilt. Cards, flowers, telephone calls to the doctor, and the insistence that nothing be spared in the care of their ailing relative all help to soothe the guilt feelings of the family members. The solicitous display of concern prior to death is a normal healthy response that helps to cushion feelings of guilt when the end finally comes.

Unfortunately, some persons work out their guilt feelings by finding fault with the care rendered to their family member. It is as if, subconsciously, vociferous complaints during the last few days of life could offset a lifetime of real or imagined neglect. The relative who finds fault with the nursing care, the doctor, and the treatment being rendered to a parent should ask himself, "Am I really only acting out my own guilt feelings?"

THINK ABOUT OTHERS IN THE FAMILY

When the death of a loved one is imminent, the heads of the family must consider the reaction to death of those about them. The demise of an elder family member ends a chapter in the family history. Teenagers who have expressed the desire should be allowed to come to the hospital, and servicemen should be given ample time to return when the death of an aged relative is imminent. The possibility of death should be mentioned to the elderly relative still at home so that the final event will not come as a shock. Before informing an older person of the death of a loved one, however, one should consult the family doctor, who will prescribe an appropriate sedative, if warranted.

RECEIVING THE NEWS

You will always remember the moment that you learn of the death of a beloved family member. The telephone may ring in the dark of the night. You may hear the words, "I'm sorry, but. . ." from a busy nurse on a strange hospital floor. You may receive the notification of death from your family physician or from a hospital resident whom you have never seen before. Death is fickle and cannot be expected to occur when you or your family physician is at the bedside.

First comes grief, a natural reaction with reparative powers; many primitive societies gather for elaborate rituals to express grief when one of the clan dies. The family member who fails to show grief at the time of death will often sink into acute depression a few days or weeks later. The family that has followed the illness closely, communicating with the physician concerning the patient's progress and the impending death, will be better able to handle its feelings when the news of death is received.

AUTOPSY

When you are notified of the death of a family member, the physician will often request permission for an autopsy—a postmortem examination of the body, particularly useful if the cause of death is uncertain. Occasionally a dispute with an insurance company can be settled only by a postmortem examination of a person suffering violent death or dying while not under the care of a physician.

During an autopsy, inspection is made of all the internal organs through incisions made in the abdomen and chest, although the examination of the brain is one part of the examination that can be omitted, if specifically requested by the family. At the time of autopsy, microscopic sections are taken of all tissues for later examination. The attending physician, who should be present at the autopsy examination, will receive a written report of all diseases found and the actual cause of death.

Hospitals are required to perform autopsies on a certain percentage of all deaths that occur within the institution in order to retain accreditation.

WHAT DO WE DO NOW?

Upon learning of the death of a family member and responding to the request for an autopsy, you will have to notify your funeral director, even if it is the middle of the night. He will arrange with the hospital to remove the deceased person either immediately or after the autopsy has been performed. The funeral director will contact the doctor to obtain a death certificate and will get the necessary burial certificate from the town or county clerk.

Upon receiving the news, the family will want to meet and discuss plans. Funeral arrangements must be made, and grieving family members must be comforted, yet the life of the family must go on.

We must be comforted knowing that, after a robust youth, productive middle years, and mellow retirement, death is nothing more than the final chapter of the story. As the tale comes to a close, the eldest must move on so that another can take his place.

Bibliography

Here is a list of books to guide further study of the health problems of aging. The recommended works reflect various facets of staying healthy after 65 and include several general home health guides, a few cookbooks, one or two volumes of historic interest, and even several medical texts. A brief discussion of each book highlights topics of special interest to the senior citizen.

Ackerknecht, Erwin H. *History and Geography of the Most Important Diseases.* New York: Hafner, 1965.
> Read the history of the diseases that have plagued mankind since the beginning of time: tuberculosis in ancient Egypt, Hippocrates' description of cancer, the malaria epidemics of Rome, and the 1918 flu disaster. Share the thrills as the champions of preventive medicine, one after another, overcome the great plagues. Here is the story of how doctors battled disease and changed the course of history.

Anderson, W. F. *Practical Management of the Elderly.* Philadelphia: F. A. Davis, 1971.
> This illustrated medical textbook describes commonsense management of geriatric problems. Intended for the health care professional, the book may also prove useful to the family caring for an ailing senior citizen.

Bond, C.B.Y.; Dobbin, E.V.; Gofman, H.F.; Jones, H.C.; & Lyon, L. *The Low Fat Low Cholesterol Diet.* Garden City, N.Y.: Doubleday, 1971.
> This multiauthor book details the dietary assault on arteriosclerosis with menus, recipes, and tables listing the fat and cholesterol content of your favorite foods. When originally published in 1951, this was the first diet guide of its type; the 1971 edition continues to be timely and informative.

Cooley, D.G. (Ed.). *Better Homes and Gardens Family Medical Health Guide.* New York: Meredith Press, 1966.
> Liberally illustrated, this multiauthor book is on the shelves of more than two million homes and libraries. The senior

citizen will read with interest the hows and whys of X rays, electrocardiographs, and laboratory tests. The easy-reading style enhances the useful facts in this fine volume.

DiCyan, Irwin & Hessman, Lawrence. *Without Prescription: A Guide to the Selection and Use of Medicines You Can Get Over-the-Counter Without Prescription, For Safe Self-Medication.* New York: Simon & Schuster, 1972.

Thousands of medications are sold without prescriptions—which to use? This book tells which patent medicines to choose and why, always remembering that the physician should be called if symptoms persist or become worse.

Edwards, Marvin H. *Hazardous to Your Health.* New Rochelle, N.Y.: Arlington House, 1972.

There are no diets or drugs in this frankly partisan text, which explodes the myth of a "health care crisis in America." Through painstaking research and vivid exposition, the author points out the virtues of America's health care system and discusses the hidden dangers of currently proposed legislation.

Fishbein, M.J. *The Handy Home Medical Adviser and Concise Medical Encyclopedia.* Garden City, N.Y.: Doubleday, 1973.

This inexpensive volume by the prolific Dr. Fishbein trims away excess fat and gets right to the heart of disease prevention and treatment. Specific exercises are recommended, the significance of early symptoms is discussed, and there is a valuable first-aid section, plus an alphabetical discussion of common medical terms.

——. *The Modern Family Health Guide.* Garden City, N.Y.: Doubleday, 1967.

This comprehensive reference book features discussions of health problems grouped by organ systems, plus a 560-page encyclopedia section. Dr. Fishbein's text is supplemented by the contributions of other well-known medical authors.

——. *Modern Home Medical Advisor.* Garden City, N.Y.: Doubleday, 1969.

This Dr. Fishbein tome is particularly well illustrated and contains a wealth of information as do the other volumes of this series. Of particular interest to the senior citizen will be the author's discussion of regular health checkups and disease prevention.

Frank, Stanley. *The Sexually Active Man Past 40.* New York: Macmillan, 1968.

> Problems of the climacteric, taboos, and waning potency are examined. Senior citizens will particularly enjoy Chapter 11: "Oh, to Be Seventy Again!" It begins: "Society's antagonism to sex in the old can be summed up in seven words: virility at twenty-five is lechery at sixty-five."

Gaver, J.R. *The Complete Directory of Medical and Health Services.* New York: Award Books, 1970.

> This unique paperback book tells where help can be found and how to get it. For example, there are lists of renal dialysis centers, sources of aid for the alcoholic, societies for the blind, and cancer rehabilitation services. The book not only gives the names and addresses of agencies and institutions, but discusses their particular merits and limitations.

Havighurst, C.C. *Health Care.* Dobbs Ferry, N.Y.: Oceana Publications, 1972.

> This 452-page book examines present and potential problems in Federal health care, including the Medicare program for senior citizens—its good points and bad. Discussed also are problems of access to health care, group practice, paying for medical care, and the specter of national health insurance.

Hertzler, Arthur E. *The Horse and Buggy Doctor.* New York: Harper & Brothers, 1938.

> Here's a nostalgic look at medical care at the turn of the century by the intrepid Dr. Hertzler, who made his calls in a buggy, armed with his black bag of instruments, wirecutters, and a Colt six-shooter.

Hyman, Harold T. *The Complete Home Medical Encyclopedia.* New York: Avon Books, 1971.

> Regularly revised and updated since first published in 1963, this 832-page paperback volume contains a wealth of common sense advice. Of particular interest is the section on retirement (discussing retirementophobia, retirementitis, and

preparing for R-day) and the well-written sections discussing sexuality. Topics are arranged in encyclopedic fashion, supplemented by a top-notch index.

Kaplan, J. *Social Welfare of the Aging.* New York: Columbia University Press, 1962.
> The fifth Congress of the International Associations of Gerontology, aptly titled "Aging Around the World," produced several learned treatises. This one discusses problems shared by senior citizens in many countries.

Lewis, Faye C. *Patients, Doctors, and Families.* Garden City, N.Y.: Doubleday, 1968.
> Dr. Lewis, the first woman to receive a medical degree from Washington University, takes a disarming look at health, hospitals, relatives, and old age. As a woman approaching her 82nd birthday confided to Dr. Lewis, "There are ways of coping with infirmities. I read with a magnifying glass, walk with a walker, and sleep with a can of Miller's High Life."

Little, Billie & Thorup, Penny L. *Recipes for Diabetics.* New York: Grosset & Dunlap, 1972.
> The elderly diabetic and his family will welcome this array of mouth-watering low-carbohydrate dishes, their succulent appeal diminished not one whit by consideration of weight equivalents and food-exchange lists.

Miller, B.F., & Galton, L. *The Family Book of Preventive Medicine.* New York: Simon & Schuster, 1971.
> This 704-page volume eloquently presents the case for preventive medicine, emphasizing the importance of having regular physical examinations and building sound defenses against disease. The authoritative discussions of multiphasic screening and therapeutic agents will be of special interest to the senior citizen.

Miller, Dolcy B. *The Extended Care Facility.* New York: McGraw-Hill, 1970.
> Here is a 512-page professional guide to the organization and operation of an extended-care facility, commonly called a nursing home. An evening spent with this volume could be of

immense value to the senior citizen (or his family) faced with the prospect of entering such a facility.

Page, I.H.; Millikan, C.M.; Wright, I.S.; Weiss, E.; Crawford, E.S.; DeBakey, M.E.; & Rusk, H.A. *Strokes: How They Occur and What Can Be Done About Them.* New York: Dutton, 1961.

> Seven leading medical authorities pooled their knowledge to produce this compact volume analyzing one of the major threats to the senior citizen. How strokes occur, how they are diagnosed, how they relate to emotions, and how they are treated—all are examined. Of particular interest to many senior citizens is Dr. Rusk's illustrated Chapter 8, discussing rehabilitation following a stroke.

Palmore, Erdman. *Normal Aging.* Durham, N.C.: Duke University Press, 1970.

> This 431-page scientific treatise, supplemented with charts and diagrams, tabulates the results of a 14-year study at Duke University, covering all aspects of normal aging. Described by James M. A. Weiss in *The American Journal of Psychiatry* as "the definitive research compendium on the subject," the book views the senior citizen's problems through the eyes of the scholar, statistician, and social planner.

Pauly, Mark V. *Medical Care at Public Expense.* New York: Praeger, 1971.

> The book takes a penetrating look at applied welfare economics, including Medicare, Medicaid, the inevitable national health insurance, and other health legislation of interest to the senior citizen.

Poe, William D. *The Old Person at Your Home.* New York: Scribner's, 1969.

> In his preface, Dr. Poe says it all: "This book is intended for all who face the responsibility of caring for the elderly, but particularly for those in situations where two or more generations live together." The author has an aversion to the term senior citizen and begins by assuming that the "old person" is incapable of caring for himself. Otherwise, the 174-page book is readable and to the point.

Rosow, Irving. *Social Integration of the Aged.* New York: Macmillan Co., Free Press, 1967.

> The book examines the senior citizen's role in a jet-age society and will be of interest to politicians, sociologists, social planners, and other individuals with a professional interest in the over-65er's health and well-being.

Rossman, Isadore. *Clinical Geriatrics.* Philadelphia: Lippincott, 1971.

> Actually a medical text, this important book is listed here because it should be studied by every doctor, nurse, aide, and family caring for a geriatric patient. Many fine physicians have contributed to the 525-page text, which discusses the aging process and its clinical problems.

Stevens, Rosemary. *American Medicine and the Public Interest.* New Haven: Yale University Press, 1971.

> A scholarly footnoted text, the book traces the origins of medicine in America and details the evolution of our present health-care delivery system. Senior citizens will recall the days when medical education was hit-or-miss and the local physician may have had little more than a brief apprenticeship punctuated by an occasional didactic lecture. How this all changed and why is discussed, along with the current problems faced by the medical profession and health planners.

Taylor, Robert B. *A Primer of Clinical Symptoms.* Hagerstown, Md.: Harper & Row, 1973.

> Illness always begins with a symptom, and this book guides the home evaluation of disease symptoms, discussing possible physical changes, suspected diagnoses, and available treatment. Common symptoms of each organ system are examined, often allowing the reader to reach a diagnosis before arriving at the doctor's office. This liberally illustrated handbook is intended for the individual with abdominal pain who doesn't know whether he should look up appendicitis, peptic ulcer, or nervous stomach.

Index